A Journey in God's Sovereignty

...ard P. Belcher

Cover Photography by Lena Kittrell

ISBN 1-883265-28-2

Richbarry Press

105 River Wood Drive, Fort Mill, SC 29715

Printed in the United States of America

An Introduction to the "Journey" Theological Novels!

This is the fourteenth book in a continuing series about Ira F. Pointer and his struggles to understand and preach the truth of the Word of God. For the reader's help, a very brief summary of each book is given in this introduction to the series.

Book One, *A Journey in Grace*, finds Ira in the fall of 1970 studying for the ministry in Collegetown. His pursuit in this book becomes Calvinism---what is it and does the Bible teach it?

Book Two, *A Journey in Purity*, begins in the winter of 1971, as Ira faces the problem of impurity in the lives of his church members.

Book Three, *A Journey in Authority*, is set in the year of 1972, a few months after book two. Ira is in a new church, Unity Baptist Church. The theological search this time concerns church government---elder leadership versus congregational rule.

Book Four, *A Journey in the Spirit*, has its setting in the Spring of 1973. Ira meets Durwood Girvin, the new pastor at First Baptist Church. The doctrinal pursuit is the Holy Spirit, as he finds himself in conflict with Girvin on the subject.

Book Five, *A Journey in Inspiration*, finds its setting in the summer of 1976, as Ira heads to seminary, and finds himself unintentionally caught up in the inerrancy battle.

Book Six, *A Journey in Providence*, takes place in 1981. Ira is taking a rest, having finished the Master of Divinity degree, before further study. The book begins with the kidnapping of Dink's son, which results in Ira and Dink studying the providence of God in the book of Job, as they seek the lost son.

Book Seven, *A Journey in Eschatology*, originates during the summer of 1982. Ira faces a double challenge---to find his birth parents and to write a book on the subject of eschatology. Both pursuits prove to be much more difficult than he had anticipated.

Book Eight, *A Journey in Salvation*, commences during the fall of 1983. Ira now has joined the faculty of a seminary, where he is teaching, while he pursues doctoral studies. The doctrinal search is in the area of salvation, as Ira and Dink seek to help a fallen pastor understand the basics of true salvation.

Book Nine is titled *A Journey in Revival---True or False?* The setting is the Spring of 1985. Ira has completed his doctoral work and is still teaching at the seminary. The theological conflict concerns an end-time revival in their city.

Book Ten is titled *A Journey in Baptism*, and unfolds in the fall of 1985. Ira and one of his students discuss objectively the doctrine of baptism, with Ira setting forth a covenantal Baptist view, and the student the Paedobaptist understanding of baptism. At the same time Ira is pulled into a puzzling sniper mystery.

Book Eleven, titled *A Journey in Roman Catholicism*, takes place in the fall of 1986. Ira is accused of having written a book declaring that he is going to become a Roman Catholic, and the evidence is so persuasive that he is relieved of his duties as a professor at the Baptist Seminary. Dink disappears, as they seek to uncover this web of deceit which has engulfed them.

Book Twelve, titled *A Journey in God's Glory*, takes place in the early part of 1988. Ira encounters a pastor, who ministered for his own glory for years. But then he hits the wall, when his wife leaves him and disappears to get away from her overbearing and self-centered husband. He seeks Ira's help concerning a life and ministry for the glory of God.

Book Thirteen, *A Journey in Faith,* is set in the summer of 1989. Ira and Dink are pulled into the mystery of the elimination of all the records of a pastor and his books, even though he had spent forty-three years pastoring in a small mountain town. Many lessons on faith are learned by Ira and Dink, as they seek to find the answer to this mystery.

Book Fourteen, *A Journey in Sovereignty*, is set in the fall of 1991 into the Spring of 1992. Ira and Dink come into criticism at the seminary where they teach, because of their Calvinistic convictions. The situation becomes so serious, that it seems certain that they will lose their jobs as teachers, but they seek to react as godly men should, even when others around them do not.

Though each book is part of a continuing series, a person can read any book separately with understanding, as each plot stands as a single unit, and each theological study is independent as well. However, some characters from the previous books appear in later books as part of the plot. Therefore, a reading of the books in order will help the reader understand the characters better in the process.

Chapter 1

It was a sad day in the Fall of 1991, when it was announced that Dr. Graham, the president of the seminary where I taught, would be retiring at the end of that school year. Those of you, who are regular readers of our series of theological novels, know the close friendship that Dink and I shared with Dr. Graham. He had stood with us when others had tried to destroy our ministry and even our lives, such as in our last journey (see *A Journey in Faith*).

It was even a sadder day, when the Spring of 1992 arrived, and the end of the semester actually brought to an end his presidency. It was with a deep spirit of respect and love whereby we all said our good-byes. I had hoped he would remain in Seminary City and still be active somehow in the life of the school, but instead he and his wife were moving to the Midwest to be closer to their family.

The school had been in the process all year of seeking a new president, and at the graduation services it was announced (to my surprise and joy) that an old professor and friend of mine had been chosen to lead the school. It was Dr. Norman Sisk, who had been such a help to me, as he guided me into an understanding of the definition of Calvinism, when I was in my early years of college, even though I don't think he was a Calvinist himself (see *A Journey in Grace*). How well I remembered his gracious and kind spirit in those early days of my learning experience, and so I was looking eagerly to his coming to the seminary as its new president.

I hadn't been on campus during the days he visited for his interviews, and so I didn't get to see him before he arrived to take over his official duties as president. And since I was in and out of town in ministry during the summer, when he moved to our city and actually became the president, I didn't think I would get to see him until the faculty meetings began in the fall prior to the students arriving on campus. He had always been such a friendly and open man to meet, but then I hadn't seen him in twenty years or so. But I had no reason to think he would be any different from the time that I had known him previously.

So, when I spotted him walking across campus in the distance one day, I hurried over and cut him off, so that I could speak to him for a moment.

"Dr. Sisk! I just wanted to say hello. It's been a long time since our days together at Collegetown, when you were so helpful to me in my theological pursuits!"

He looked at me like he didn't know me, which puzzled me, so I tried again.

"Ira Pointer? One of your students at Baptist College? One to whom you were so kind as to help me in my understanding of Calvinism?" I said, as I kept offering hints.

"Oh, yes!" he finally recalled. "The young man who did become a Calvinist, so I hear! Maybe I did too good of a job explaining what a Calvinist is, in that I evidently persuaded you to become one!" he replied, but not with a smile on his face. "Someone did tell me that you were on the faculty here and had been very successful in making a lot of students into Calvinists!" he said with a smile, but I wasn't sure it was a friendly one. It seemed to be more of a smirk, that is, an insincere grin, than a friendly smile.

I didn't know quite how to react, so I smiled back and said, "Well, I have never regretted the good job you did nor the friendship you offered me in a time of need. I so much appreciated you in that you didn't try to force your view on me. The fact of the matter is, I don't know to this day what theological position you would call your own. I so appreciated your objectivity as you spoke with me and explained the various systems of theology to me. In fact, I try to emulate you in that respect, in that, though I am a Calvinist now, I want to be fair with others in their views and in the presentation of my beliefs."

"Well, Mr. Pointer, I have had something of a change of heart on that matter!" he alerted me. "There has come a revival of Calvinism in our denomination recently, and one reason I have taken the presidency of this seminary is to try to cut down on the strong influence of some of these Calvinists. Anymore, they are every where! There is even a fellowship of them in our denomination, and they meet every year to preach those doctrines. This is not the kind of a denomination I grew up in, nor is it the kind of denomination I want. Therefore, I am going to be very careful who we hire here at this school, so that we do not become overrun with men of your persuasion. I know you have been here for a long time, and that is fine with me---as long as you are careful with your Calvinism, or don't become too extreme in your views."

"Careful with my Calvinism? And don't become too extreme in my views?" I queried. "Aren't those pretty subjective statements, which are open to wide interpretations, depending on who is defining the terms?"

"Mr. Pointer, I am a Calvinist of sorts, but not the extreme Calvinist that you are! As I understand it, you possess a view that does violation to the will of man--- something I do not want on this campus!" he stated firmly.

I saw we were not getting anywhere, and that he was in a hurry, so I made a suggestion with a smile.

"Perhaps, we can meet again, as we did almost twenty years ago, and discuss the nature of a true Calvinist!"

Chapter 2

Dr. Sisk didn't answer my smiling suggestion. We just shook hands and went our different ways. But I couldn't help but wonder what the implications of his statements were for my future ministry here at the seminary. Also, I couldn't believe such a change could take place in a man in just twenty years! He had gone from being an open and friendly individual to a serious and unfriendly person (at least to me), and he seemed to have an axe to grind against Calvinism, even though he said he was a Calvinist of sorts, whatever that could possibly mean.

I decided to stop by Dink's office and see what he thought of this strange turn of events. He listened carefully, and then offered his usual blunt opinion.

"Wow, Preacha! It sounds ta me like he's comin' at ya wid a chainsaw!"

I laughed at Dink's expression, and then commented, "Well, thanks Dink! That sure does encourage me!"

"Well, if he's comin' after you, den he's comin' after me, too, cause we'se floatin' along in da same Calvinist canoe!" he stated unflinchingly. "Guess we's both either goin' ta ride dat canoe down together or da Lord's gonna sink his boat, if he tries ta do sometin' against God's will!"

That gave me some encouragement, as it reminded me of our previous "journey in faith!" We decided to let things remain as they were and had been all our teaching days at the school---eight years or so. If Dr. Sisk had a bone to pick with me or us, then let him introduce the matter. Until then we would just wait on the Lord and do His will for our lives.

It didn't take long, however, for the issue to resurface once more, at least, it seemed to be resurfacing. Each time

I looked up in my classes during the first weeks of that semester, I saw the Dean of Faculty present. It went on like that for about a month. The strange thing was that in my years of teaching at the seminary, no dean had ever visited my classes. I told myself not to jump to conclusions, because that would be a proper thing for a dean to do, especially a new one---to get acquainted with his faculty members in the classroom and learn their strengths and weaknesses. And he was the new dean of the faculty, right along with a new seminary president. When I asked Dink, he said the dean was monitoring his classes as well.

But in the passing of the next several weeks, as I kept my ears open, I became convinced that the dean was not monitoring anyone else's classes except ours. This did strike me as rather unusual, but not an impossible situation, unless Dink and I were being singled out because of our theological views. The shocker came when I was called into the dean's office for a conference. Before I went to meet with him, I called Dink, and he said he was scheduled to see the dean also right after lunch. With some reservations I made my way across campus to the meeting.

"Dr. Pointer!" the new dean, Dr. Welsh, began. "I just wanted to alert you that you may not be given another contract for teaching here at the seminary next year. I'm giving you plenty of time, so you can think of other possible avenues of service for the Lord!"

I must admit, I had not expected this. I thought he might want to discuss theology with me, and let me present my position. Quickly, I thought of a question, which might reveal something further concerning the reason for this possibility of non-renewal of my contract. If it was doctrinal, I wanted to know that very clearly.

"Oh!" I stated as calmly as I could, "I would expect you to give me a reason for the negative decision and an honest reason at that!" As I said this, I had to admit that I had never expected he would give the reason he did, and I really wondered if it came from him or from the top.

"Well, you seem to be lacking in communicative skills," he offered lamely. "I am sorry! I know you have been here a number of years, and that this is something that should have been dealt with some time ago. But there is no reason to prolong the matter. Dr. Sisk wants to build a strong faculty here, and he sees the theology department as one of our weakest areas."

"Does he see our theology department weak because of its lack of ability to communicate or because of the theological outlook of one of the professors?" I asked bluntly.

"Oh, no, it's like I said, you are a poor communicator!"

"Dr. Welsh, I can hardly believe that! From what basis do you draw that conclusion? From my class evaluations? From my invitations to preach regularly in different churches all over the state and in many other states? I think if you will check, you will find that I'm preaching somewhere on the weekends and even sometimes through the week more than any other faculty member. Not bad, for a poor communicator! Sir, you know that you do not have the evidence to support your conclusion, and I think that if this claim would get out, you and the new president, might very well become the laughing stock of the campus."

He sat there quiet and speechless. That's what happens when you are forced to carry the water for someone else. These were not his convictions nor conclusions, but Dr. Sisk's. But I wasn't finished.

"Is that what you are going to tell Dink also?" I noted with a laugh. "That he is a poor communicator too? And might I ask you, how many other faculty members are you not going to rehire for that reason? Perhaps, even a more basic question is this: how many classes of other faculty members have you even visited this semester besides mine and Dink's? Doesn't that tell you (it does me) that you have not been honest with me in this matter, but that Dink and I have been singled out for theological reasons? Should not the hallmark of a new dean and president be honesty? Can you sit there before our God and tell me you are being completely honest with me now?"

By this time his face had all the color flushed out of it! He looked like he had the face of a dead man! He finally said, "Well, let me talk to the president, and get back to you!"

I thanked him, as I walked out the door! He tried to make a similar gesture, but he knew that he had gotten caught with his hand not only in the cookie jar, but stuck in it, and he had no one to turn to for help to get it out. I made a beeline to Dink's office, and I told him I was neither a prophet nor the son of a prophet, but I would venture to say his afternoon appointment would soon be canceled, and we would never hear of this false accusation again. What they would do next, though, I would not try to predict.

Sure enough, as I waited in Dink's office, the phone call did come to cancel his meeting. It wasn't even from the dean, but from his secretary. Now we would just wait and see if we would ever hear of this "you're not a good communicator" thing again.

Maybe now the president would be willing to discuss with me the nature of a true Calvinist before he fired me!

Chapter 3

A month or so went by and we hadn't heard anything from the dean or the president. I had seen them both several times, but not a word about their "poor communicator" statement. And when I saw them, you would have thought nothing had ever happened of that sort. Finally, one day the president flagged me down on campus, and suddenly he was all smiles as he spoke to me.

"Dr. Pointer! I want you to do a favor for me!"

When he stopped after that one sentence, I was at a loss as to what to say. Finally I offered, "Well, I'll do my best to oblige you, if I possibly can during this busy time of the semester!"

"I would like for you to write a paper and set forth your views of Calvinism!" he stated, and then stopped again with that brief announcement.

"How many pages are required in this paper?" I asked, as I stated the obvious question, wondering if he knew the busy schedule I kept, as did all his faculty members.

"Oh, I would say thirty pages---maybe a little longer!" he said with another smile.

"And what is the purpose of this paper? That is, what will be done with this paper?" I queried again, not wanting to be sucked into something that would disrupt my semester and my family.

"Well, I think we can use it as the basis of determining whether you will be given a new contract or not!" he finally admitted.

I couldn't resist saying it, and almost before I knew it the words came out, as I bluntly challenged him, "Oh, then you have given up on the poor communicator thing, as the means of evaluating me and Dink as teachers?"

It was obvious on his face that he didn't like that jab, and he weakly said, "Oh, that wasn't my idea, anyway! So, how about it? A paper or what?"

I wondered again what he meant by "Or what?" Did he want me to make a suggestion on how he could evaluate me, or was he saying that it was write a paper or hit the road! I decided to be brave and make a suggestion.

"I'll tell you what I'd prefer, and you can raise the flag on my idea, and we will salute it or you can shoot it down."

He didn't stop me, and so I said, "I prefer a number of meetings with you where we could discuss various aspects of the subject of Calvinism face to face. This way you could get to know my heart, as well as my views, and there could be a friendly give and take in the process, which would let you see my true views, rather than some preconceived concepts of what kind of Calvinist I am."

He seemed to warm up to that idea, and after discussing some ground rules for our meetings, he agreed. But then I pressed him a little further.

"Dr. Sisk, if you are considering an evaluation of Dink, just as you are of me, we might as well include him in these meetings, rather than evaluate him in another manner."

At first he seemed a little cold to that possibility, as he said, "Well, you know, Dink is another subject. He's really not too bright, is he? And his speech is atrocious! And to think he is actually on our faculty here!"

"Sir, don't underestimate Dink! I warn you! If you do, you will come up with egg all over your face! He's brilliant---one of the smartest men I have ever known!"

"Dink? Mr. Evangelist Dink? Mr. Gangster Dink?" he said laughing out loud.

"Careful, sir. He knows as much theology as I do, and I would venture to say as much as you do. Maybe more!"

Chapter 4

Dr. Sisk and I parted with him scratching his head over my last statement concerning Dink. He still couldn't believe it, but he did agree to let Dink meet with us and to make that process the determination of the renewal of his contract also. We were going to meet once a week for an hour or more, if necessary, and work through the various aspects of the Calvinistic system. He said he was interested in all I would say, and I was also interested to find out what he meant when he said he was a Calvinist of sorts.

As I met with Dink and explained it all to him, his eyes lit up and he said with some glee, "Preacha, dis is right up our alley! He don't know dat we'se been doin' dis kinda study fer some years now!"

I didn't have the heart to tell Dink what Dr. Sisk had said about him, not that it would have bothered him. People had been underestimating him and his intelligence and criticizing his language ever since I had known him. I had no doubt when the showdown came, he would be able to carry his own in the theology discussions. I thought to myself, maybe I had better save my pity for poor Dr. Sisk, since he's never tangled with the Dink man before!

As I walked across the campus, I was shocked when one of my students came up to me and asked if he could pose a personal question to me. I told him, yes, but to remember I was not obligated to answer personal questions.

"Is it true that you are not going to be on the faculty next year? There's a rumor going around the campus that you and Dink are not going to be given new contracts for the next year, and, honestly, Dr. Pointer, that could cause a real stir if it proves to be true!" he warned.

I smiled, and then said, "Can't answer either way! Too personal! What if I was going to resign and then didn't? Then, you and whoever else thinks he knows something, would have chased a rabbit down the wrong path! Just put it in the Lord's hands and His will shall be done!"

I didn't lie to him, but I just put it all in the form of a question to quiet any potential problem among the students. I did have a strong backing on campus, and though he hadn't mentioned Dink, he did too. Dr. Sisk didn't know it, but somebody had a mole in his office, who had leaked this information, because it hadn't come from Dink or me---not even our wives knew about it. It had to be Dr. Sisk or Dr. Welsh or someone in their offices.

Then, as I got back to my office, finally, and was entering it, the professor across the hall, Dr. Singleton asked if he could speak to me. He was younger than I was, and had been at the school for about two years.

"Dr. Pointer, is it true that the new president is going to crack down on anyone who is a Calvinist?" he blurted out.

I thought to myself, what is going on here? Does everyone on campus really know about this matter? Finally, I asked him the expected question.

"Who told you that?" I spoke almost demandingly.

"Well, I'm kind of sworn to secrecy! But it really concerns me, because I am a Calvinist, and with a new baby coming, and having been here only two years, I must admit that it kind of scares me!" he replied.

I was sorry then that I might have come down on him too forcefully. So I tried to encourage him.

"Dr. Singleton, I wouldn't worry about it for now. If something does change, and I am not saying that it will, remember your belief in a sovereign God, Who is working all things after the council of His own will!"

Chapter 5

As I left Dr. Singleton and went on into my office, I couldn't help but remember what a blessing this verse, which very clearly and succinctly speaks of God's sovereignty over all things, had comforted my heart through the years. "He is working all things after the counsel of His own will!" (Ephesians 1:11). I tried to imagine how different my perspective on life would be, if I did not believe this truth of God's sovereignty.

What a basket case I might have been all through my life and its many experiences, if I did not have the absolute assuring confidence that HE WAS a sovereign God. This guarantees me that He has been in control of everything that came to pass in my life and in the life of my family and in the world in which I live. And I can be assured that His sovereignty was not a temporary thing, but a constant in my life and in all the unfolding events around me.

I sat on the couch in my office and meditated on that fact, and sensed the peace and comfort of the truth. I prayed for my younger colleague, that this doctrine might be a reality to him during this year, which was before us, and in face of whatever the president of the seminary had in mind concerning us as Calvinists.

I then mediated on the previous verse and other verses, which stressed His sovereignty, such as the following:

1. EPHESIANS 1:11

God is spoken of as the One *"Who worketh all things after the counsel of his own will."*

> According to the setting forth or purpose
>   of Him who works all things effectually
>   after the counsel
>   or the pleasure of His desire or will

2. PSALM 33:22

The counsel of the Lord stands forever, the thoughts of his heart to all generations.

> His counsel, plan or purpose
>   abides, is appointed, is affirmed
>   is perpetual or eternal or forever
> The purpose or thoughts
>   of His will, heart, intellect
>   abides, is appointed is affirmed
>   to all generations or ages

3. PSALM 115:3

But our God is in the heavens; he hath done whatsoever he hath pleased.

> But our God (*Elohim*) is in the heavens
> He has accomplished, advanced, governed, ruled
>   everything---as He willed or would or pleased

4. DANIEL 4:35

And all the inhabitants of the earth are reputed as nothing; and he doeth according to his will in the army of heaven, and among the inhabitants of the earth, and none can stay his hand, or say unto him, What doest thou?

> And all the inhabitants of the earth---
>> all men and creatures---
>>> are regarded, considered, or esteemed
>>>> as nothing
> And He executes, moves, works
>> according as He wishes or pleases or wills
>>> in the army of heaven
>>>> and among the inhabitants of the earth
> And no one or none
>> can or is able to stop or stay or impale
>>> His hand or power
> Nor can anyone say, ask or command unto Him
>> What are you doing?
>> Why are you executing things thusly?
>> Why are you working this way?

5. PROVERBS 8:15

By me kings reign and princes declare justice...

> By God kings ascend the throne, rule, or reign
>> and princes or rulers decree or govern
>>> with justice or righteousness

6. PROVERBS 21:1

The king's heart is in the hand of the Lord, like the rivers of water; he turneth it withersoever he will.

The king's heart, feelings or intellect
is in the hand of the Lord (*Jehovah*)
like rivers or channels of water
He bends them, turns them, causes them to yield
accordingly, in what manner, howsoever
He desires, favors, wills or would

7. ISAIAH 14:27

For the Lord of hosts hath purposed, and who shall disannul it? And his hand is stretched out, and who shall turn it back.

For or now the Lord (*Jehovah*) of hosts
has determined or purposed and Who shall
cause it to cease
annul it or change it
make it of no effect
cause it to fail
make it utterly void
cause it to cease
defeat it
And His hand
is outstretched and extended and is gone forth
and who shall turn it back
and who shall cause it to return or retreat
and who shall hinder it

8. PROVERBS 19:21

There are many devices in a man's heart; nevertheless, the counsel of the Lord, that shall stand.

> There are many cunning works
>> or curious works
>>> or imaginations
>>>> or intentions
>>>>> in the heart of a man
>> nevertheless the purpose or plan
>>> of the Lord (*Jehovah*)
>>>> shall stand, abide, endure, or remain
>>>> (whatever man plans)

9. PSALM 76:10

Surely the wrath of man shall praise thee; the remainder of wrath thou shalt restrain.

> Surely the anger or hot displeasure or wrath of man
>> shall bring worship or praise to God
> The remainder of the anger or wrath of man
>> God shall restrain, control, or hold back

10. ACTS 2:23

Him (Christ), being delivered by the determinate counsel and foreknowledge of God, ye have taken, and by wicked hands have crucified and slain.

> that One (Christ) was delivered or surrendered over
> by the appointed decree
>> and by the previously determined counsel
>>> (or by the ordained will of God)
> you have taken and by lawless hands
>> have crucified and killed him

Note---some would want to translate the first of the above phrases to refer to God's appointed decree and the second one to refer to His foreknowledge. Actually, the second word in the Greek, which is translated by many as "foreknowledge" can mean either foreknowledge or foreordination. Thus, we must look for some reason why we would translate it one way or the other. There is a rule in Greek, known as the Granville Sharp rule, which says that if we have an article (the) with a noun connected to another noun with the word "and" (Greek *kai*), it speaks of the same thing, if the second noun does not have the article. If it has the article with both nouns, then it is speaking of two different things. Thus, we have translated the two words as referring to the same thing in different terms (appointed decree and previously determined counsel), rather than seeing them as referring to God's appointed decree in the first noun and to His foreknowledge in the second instance. Our conclusion is that the author is not speaking of foreordination here in the first word and foreknowledge in the second noun, but of God's foreordination in both words.

11. ACTS 4:27-28

For of a truth against thy holy child, Jesus, whom thou hast anointed, both Herod and Pontius Pilate, with the nations, and the people of Israel, were gathered together, to do whatever thy hand and thy counsel determined before to be done.

> This verse says very clearly that Herod and Pilate
>   along with the nations and people of Israel
>   were gathered together against Jesus
> to do whatever God's hand
>   ordained beforehand
>   predetermined
>   preordained
>   predestinated
>   to be done

As I sat and reviewed these verses, one by one, I came to tears as I realized anew the unfathomable depth of God's sovereignty. But it was not only the reality of God's sovereignty, but the extent by which I was held in His hands every moment and every hour and every second of every day of my feeble little life!

I made a list of all that God's sovereignty included according to these verses.

1. God's decree concerns everything that comes to pass in my life.

2. God's decree does not allow any chance-happenings or accidents to come into my life.

3. God's decree extends to all events and creatures in the world as well as to me.

4. God's decree extends to all history of the nations and all the events therein.

5. God's decree extends to every aspect of every man's life.

6. God's decree includes the life and actions of every believer.

7. God's decree includes the life and actions of every lost man and every wicked deed, though God is not the author of sin.

As I sat and wept, I realized there were a lot of questions to answer concerning God's sovereignty and man's responsibility, but there is no question about the basic premise of the Bible and the doctrine of our God--- God is in control of all things. All thoughts of God and what takes place in this world and in man's life must begin with that truth. Yes, there are many other questions to ask and answer, some of which may be screaming out at us, even now in light of what I have just said. But this truth must be settled once and for all in a person's life with no ifs, ands, or buts about it. Without this truth man would be up the creek without a paddle and out to sea without a sail.

As one of my favorite writers wrote some years ago:

Who is regulating affairs on this earth today---God, or the Devil? That God reigns supreme in Heaven, is generally conceded; that He does so over this world, is almost universally denied---if not directly, then indirectly.....Throughout Christendom, with an almost negligible exception, the theory is held that man is a "free agent", and therefore, lord of his fortunes and the determiner of his destiny (Pink, *Sovereignty of God*, Baker ed., p. 11).

In light of the Bible, how can men seek to rob God of His sovereignty in any way? But they do, as we shall see!

Chapter 6

I was suddenly jolted out of my meditations on the sovereignty of God by a knock on my study door. It was two of my students, which was not unusual, who had signed up for lunch with me that day. I hadn't even noticed their names on my sign-up sheet on the door. As I looked puzzled when I saw them, they smiled and pointed to the door, and we had a good laugh about absent-minded professors. They had been in a number of my classes. Some students, when they found a professor whom they liked, would sign up for as many of his classes as they could. These were two such "buddies." As a result, we had grown close over their years at the school, as they were now seniors. Their names were Roman Sandusky and Philip Malone.

As we made our way out to the car, we joked and laughed, and unexpectedly picked up Dink, as he was walking across campus to the school cafeteria. He at first refused to go with us, thinking that he might be horning in on our private meeting. But when they hounded him to come along also, he really wasn't hard to convince, just as long as he knew he was not butting in on a personal gathering. Roman finally sealed it with the statement that they had wanted to go to lunch for a long time with their two favorite professors.

After ordering our food, things suddenly got very quiet and then serious, though all I did was ask how their classes were coming along.

"Do you really want me to answer that question?" cautioned Philip.

"I'm game!" I stated, and then turned to Dink for his approval, not even dreaming what was coming next.

"Well, the newest professor took a few pot shots at you in class several days ago!" he noted.

"Pot shots? At me? I hardly know the man! You didn't misunderstand him, did you?" I asked.

"Well, let me tell you what he said, and you tell me if there was any possibility that I misunderstood him!" Philip offered. I nodded for him to proceed, and he added that he had it on tape!

I was reluctant to listen, fearing that it might be some gossip, but after some thought, I concluded that it was something I needed to hear, if a brother had something against me.

"He said you were a hyper-Calvinist and not a true Calvinist, but he never defined the terms. He spent the rest of the class period trying to argue that he was a five point Calvinist, but not a hyper like you are! But it seemed to me that he was an Arminian---a five point Arminian at that!"

At first I laughed and said, "I don't even know the man! This is his first semester to teach here, and we have spoken casually a few times, but other than that we haven't even had more than three sentences in one of our conversations! How does he think that he knows what I believe in any area of theology, let alone, that I am or am not a true Calvinist?"

"But that's not all!" Roman continued. "He said there was going to be a shake-up of the faculty this year, and the new president was going to rebuild it on the basis of the historic Baptist position of moderate Calvinism. I took that to mean that the school was going to replace any professor, who insisted on maintaining any view of Calvinism, that he didn't think was in agreement with his and the new president's view! And that ruffled a lot of feathers in his class, though no one spoke up to tell him that! Some of us talked after class about what we could do to let the administration know of our theological commitment to these great doctrines of grace. But even worse, as the word scattered on campus, some of the students said that they were going to transfer to another school, if anything like that actually happened."

Then Philip grabbed the conversation again, and he was as upset as Roman, when he said, "Some of us are talking about organizing and protesting peacefully to let the administration and board of trustees know what is going on, and that not all students are satisfied with it. There was and had been perfect peace and harmony in discussing theology on our campus the whole time we have been here, without any of this cut-throat mentality of the Arminians are out to get the Calvinists and vice versa. Neither has there been any tension between groups who claimed to be different kinds of Calvinists. Dr. Pointer, what can we do?"

My answer was short and simple, "Nothing! Except to pray and leave the matter in the Lord's hands. Yes, by all means, engage in conversation, but be sure and keep it low-key and as objective as possible and as theological discussions between friends---not enemies. Do not try to make anyone a Calvinist by Arminian means of high pressure and any strong armed tactics of any kind of threat or force. If others want to do that, let them do so. Just keep your cool, and tell all that agree with you to do the same, and God will work it out according to His will and for His glory. Isn't that what we should understand to be the proper Biblical procedure, whatever our view in this matter?"

"Kinda simple, ain't it?" chimed in Dink, "when youse believes da Bible ta be da Worda God an' ya wants ta be like Jesus!"

Chapter 7

It was several days before the president and Dink and I got together for our first meeting for the purpose of discussing Calvinism. Since I was responsible for presenting my view, I began by a thorough presentation of the doctrine of God's sovereignty over all things as a basic Biblical doctrine. I used much of the material I had generated in my meditations, after my conversation with Dr. Singleton in his concern for the shake-up in the faculty, which was being rumored around the campus.

When I was finished, Dr. Sisk said with a smile (one of his sly smiles), "Oh, I believe God is sovereign over all things! Now, doesn't that make me a Calvinist?"

I smiled back with my best smirky smile and said, "Well, that depends on what you mean by that statement!"

I thought to myself, how sad it is that so many theologians want to redefine their terms, just so they can fool people or even themselves into thinking they are something they are not. Like the theologian who says he believes in the inspiration of the Bible. Yeah! Whose view of inspiration---the dynamic view or the neo-orthodox view or the Biblical view of verbal inspiration?

"I believe that God is sovereign over all things in accordance with His predestination and foreknowledge!" he offered once more.

"Again, what does that mean?" I replied. "Is He sovereign over all things according to His predestination of all things or is He sovereign over all things in accordance with His foreknowledge or prescience of all things? Or would your view be that sovereignty is based on both foreordination and foreknowledge, seen as one unit of God's mind, which cannot be separated? The problem with that view is that either way you cut the cake, you must give preference to one or the other. Either God's decrees are based on His predestination of all things or God's decree of all things is based on His foreknowledge of all things. That is to say, 1) God either decreed all things which come to pass based upon the fact of His predestination of all things and, therefore, predestination (foreordination) is the foundation of His decrees; 2) or He decreed all things which come to pass based on His foreknowledge or prescience of how He knew they would come to pass, and that is the basis of His predestination of all things.

"I say again that trying to unite these two into one view and claim to say that God's decrees are based on both His foreordination and His foreknowledge at the same time is very confusing," I continued. "And I will add that the one who takes such a view, usually before his theologizing is over, opts for one side or the other---more often than not to the side of God's decrees being based on His prescience or foreknowledge. That view says that God took a long look down through the corridors of time and saw who would choose Him by their free will, and so He choose them by election from eternity past.

"But let me ask you the more basic question or questions," I offered, "which will tell me which way you go in your view of the basis of God's decrees. Do you believe God is sovereign in everything except the matter of man's will? That is, do you think if man's will is not free that God's saving him would have to be a forcing, coercing or violation of man's will?"

Slowly and carefully he said, "I believe that God is sovereign over all things, including His sovereignty over His decree to create a man with a free will; and, along with that, His sovereignty to decree that He would save any man, who by the exercise of his free will, would put his faith and trust in Jesus Christ as the only Lord and Savior!"

"Sir, you have just destroyed your claim to be any kind of a Calvinist in that your statement denies all the five points of Calvinism! You are not a Calvinist of sorts! You are not a modified or even a moderate Calvinist! You are an Arminian! You don't believe in the sovereignty of God over all things!" I said with a friendly smile this time.

With this statement even Dink blinked! I don't know if he thought I had come on too strong with my bold statement, or if he himself didn't think my statement was true, though I had no doubts about his being a Calvinist.

"Well, let me explain that statement before we bring this first session to a close." I offered again. "Taking the five points of Calvinism according to the Calvinist acrostic of TULIP (Total Depravity, Unconditional Election, Limited Atonement, Irresistible Grace and the Perseverance of the Saints, I will show you my conviction on the subject.

1. If a person believes a man has a free will in the sense that he can in some way choose God, even with the help of God's grace, or reject God and His grace, then he doesn't believe in TOTAL DEPRAVITY. He believes in a partial depravity with a synergistic plan of salvation (God and man cooperate to produce salvation), not the monergistic view of Calvinism (salvation is of the Lord). Total depravity speaks of a spiritual inability, but this view gives man the ability to choose God or reject Him. That is not total depravity!

2. If a person believes God's sovereignty does not extend to man's will and God's ability to control man's will, and if man is the final power of choice, when it comes

to salvation, even if aided by divine grace, then he does not believe in UNCONDITIONAL ELECTION. The condition of man's power and ability of choice (God elects those who will choose Him) has become the condition of God's choice in election and election is not a sovereign unconditional choice by God.

3. If a person believes God's sovereignty does not extend to man's will in salvation, and that man's choice is the final determination of salvation, then the atonement could not have been a particular atonement. It would have to be a general atonement, so that all men with their ability to chose to be saved, could be saved or could not be saved, depending on their will, which rules out the possibility of a PARTICULAR atonement. The general atonement guarantees the salvation of no man, but only makes the salvation of all men possible, which requires a general atonement. The limited or particular atonement guarantees the salvation of the elect.

4. If God is not sovereign over salvation because man has the final choice by his power, though aided by God, in the matter of whether or not he does or does not want to be saved, that means saving grace is resistible, which eliminates the doctrine of IRRESISTIBLE GRACE.

5. If a man's will is as free as the above declarations of Arminians make it to be, and man can choose to reject salvation, even when it is presented by grace through the power of the Holy Spirit, or receive it as he wills and wishes, then his will is also free to reject salvation after he has received it, for man's will again could never be forced by God to do something, according to

Arminians. Would this not include God forcing him to remain a Christian, if he did not want to do so? Some even say that the denial of man's free will dehumanizes man---that is, if man did not have a free will, he would cease to be man and become a robot. So are they saying that man has a free will until he is saved, but then loses it at salvation? Does he then become a dehumanized robot? Would not eternal security and the perseverance of the saints, according to this view, deny a man the possession of a free will? He must remain saved! Would a saved man have less of a humanity (free will is basic to humanity according to this view), than a lost and depraved sinner? Does anyone really want to say that salvation takes away our humanity even at this point? Thus, there is a denial of the doctrine of the PERSEVERANCE OF THE SAINTS.

"Do you have all of that written down!" Dr. Sisk then asked me. And then with another smile, which I didn't know how to read again, he said, "My, we sure did create a monster back there at Baptist College, when we discussed the doctrines of Calvinism---though we never mentioned any of these things you've just stated. We only dealt with the more simple ideas of Calvinism!"

I wondered if I had sealed my doom at the seminary by that long statement, which showed Dr. Sisk that he was not a Calvinist, but an Arminian. I had to speak again.

"Dr. Sisk, it matters not to me what a man believes in these areas of theology. I teach theology not to make converts to a system, but so that students can understand the various systems, and then make a choice of their own as to which one is Biblical. In the process I seek to show the claimed Biblical evidence for each view, and I have learned that when presented with clarity the Biblical view or true Calvinist view wins out. But can we not see how befuddled a student becomes, when we redefine terms and falsely accuse someone of being something theologically that he is not, which is what is so often done with Calvinists? And does it not become even more confusing when Arminians begin to try to redefine the terms to make themselves appear to be Calvinists or Calvinistic, when they are not?

"My concern in being here today and going over my views with you is that we be honest in our statements and clear in our definitions, and not claim to be something that we are not? If that costs me my job, so be it!"

I didn't know what to make of his reaction to that statement. He only said, "We have a lot to think about now and in the days to come! Dink, you didn't say anything in this discussion? Don't you have something to add? You surely don't agree with your mentor on this, do you?"

"All I'd like ta add is dat if salvation had been up ta my will, I'da still been lost! Da Preacha here presented da gospel ta me an a buncha my gang buddies back before I got saved, an if it'd been upta me, I'd still be back der wid my buddies in da underworld. But God reached down inta dat sordid messa da crime world, an' He saved me an a few others. I can't believe dat da difference between me an dose buddies, who's still lost, is dat I chose Jesus by my power, an dey didn't. It was God's grace and nothin' else!

"If salvation's da way you say, Dr. President, den you can't pray fer men ta be saved, cause God ain't gonna overcome der wills an bring dem ta Jesus, cause accordin' ta you He can't!!! So why does ya pray? Man is da decidin' power an' factor in salvation. God can only sit by an' wait and hope fer men ta exercise der wills by der own power in order ta get saved. Dat ain't Biblical salvation!"

Chapter 8

As we walked back to our offices, Dink made a comment, which amused me, but which was surely true, when he said, "Preacha, you sure flushed out a lotta theological ducks back der, dat may take us all year ta shoot down! Deys gonna make da theological atmosphere around Dr. Sisk's head as thick as skeeters on a hot night in Carolina! He may never get dem all chased away!"

"Yes, I know what you mean, Dink. We could have discussions on some of the issues we touched till Jesus comes. So where do we go next in our discussions with him? And, by the way, thanks for the support you gave at the end. You presented the real-life application of the doctrine, which we believe. But we touched so many other issues, didn't we?"

"Yeah, Preacha! Da will of man---free will an all dat related stuff! Da state of man after da fall! Was he free before da fall an still free after da fall? Or was he free before da fall, but bound in da will after da fall? How did da falla man affect Adam an' us! What does we mean by total depravity? Or unconditional election? Or limited atonement? Or irresistible grace? Or da perseverance of da saints? What does da Arminians believe 'bout all dat stuff too? Boy, Preacha, I'se sure glad you's da one picken da route we's gonna take in da next study!"

As we parted I simply said, "Yeh, I'll bet you are!"

But then as the week passed, it became quite clear where we needed to go next in our discussions. The issue was the sovereignty of God and the freedom or free will of man in relationship to God's decrees. What kind of a will did man have? Total freedom without limitation? Or freedom with limitation? If limitation, what kind and how much limitation? But most importantly, what does the Bible say about it? And what effect did the fall have on man's freedom, if any?

Thus, I began to meditate and think more deeply concerning this subject. I had theology notes on all those areas, and could have pulled them out to make my job very easy. But I wanted this to be fresh thinking on the subject in relation to where we were in the context of our study with Dr. Sisk, and not just a canned presentation of some years past. I wanted to anticipate the questions he or anyone else might raise, if they were involved in such a discussion. As a result, I came up with the following outline and notes.

1. It is true that most believers want to be able to say that God is sovereign. But the question of man's freedom becomes to them a problem, in that they have to seek to maintain the sovereignty of God, which the Bible teaches, while at the same time deal with the matter of man and the condition of his will before a sovereign God. Is man's will free or not, and in what sense is his will free, if one wants to argue man's freedom in light of a sovereign God?

2. Calvinists would say that before the fall man's will was free to either choose God or sin, and man chose to sin. But with that choice there came a change in the nature of man, and he now possesses a nature of sin. This is why he needs a new birth (John 3:3). He is spiritually dead (Ephesians 2:1). Spiritual death includes a spiritually blind mind---no man can understand the things of God (Romans 3:11) in the spiritual sense of understanding. He possesses a will that is enslaved to

sin, as no man seeks after God in his own strength and power (Romans 3:11), until he is enabled and empowered by God. There is a sense in which the Calvinist would say that man's will is free, in that man is free to act within the confines of his nature of sin. But he is not free to act outside the confines of his nature of sin in the areas of understanding God or choosing God or even desiring God. One cannot ignore the fall and the present condition of man as a sinner, for man acts and reacts within the reality of choices made as one who has the fallen nature of a sinner.

4. Arminians would say that man did fall in Adam, but the fall still left him with the ability to choose God, as God enables him by grace. But man can also reject the grace of God, for he possesses a free will, damaged by the fall and deadened by the fall also, but not to the point where he is incapable of exercising his will in choosing God by faith in the matter of salvation. He can choose God by the presence of prevenient grace, or he can reject that grace and God with it.

5. For Calvinists God's grace is an overcoming and overpowering grace which brings a man from spiritual death to life (the new birth) first, and then man is given the gifts of repentance and faith. The work of God's grace in the life of a man is not just to bring man to a certain point in his life, and then he takes over and produces the faith to save himself. But rather the grace and power of God regenerates, enlightens, woos and brings a man to the place where he wants and can and will respond gladly to the efficacious call of the Spirit to salvation. This is not force, nor coercion, nor a

violation of a man's will. This is a joyful and grateful and desirous response to God, Whom he now has come to love and desire by the power of the new birth.

6.   Arminians often try to picture this efficacious call of the elect by God to salvation as force or a violation of man's will. They seem to picture it as if God grabs a man by the collar and says, "I am going to save you," while the man replies, "But I don't want to be saved! Leave me alone!" But God drags him across the line of salvation by force and coercion, even to the violation of his will telling him, "I have to save you---you're one of my elect!" And then when the man gets across the line of salvation, he still spits in God's face and says, "I told you I didn't want to be saved, and I meant it! So why did you save me? You forced me! You violated my will! You coerced me, and I don't like it and I will never like it!" Would not that be a description of God forcing a man to salvation? Of coercing a man to come to Christ? A violation of his will? But that is not Calvinism!

7.   Neither is the above what Calvinists mean by irresistible grace! God's grace in saving His elect is kind and enlightening, teaching the man who he is and who God is, all through the Holy Spirit by the power of God's Word. When God has finished His work of enlightening a man and teaching a man and wooing a man and calling a man, the man at some point in the working of God has become a new man by means of the power of God in regeneration. He, therefore, willingly and joyfully responds to the gracious call of the Holy Spirit, as He understands as never before how

sinful he is and how much he needs Jesus Christ, the only Savior, and that he cannot save himself. He understands that salvation is only by the grace of God!

As I had been speaking, I tried to read the reaction of Dr. Sisk to the presentation, but to be honest I drew a blank. I couldn't tell the difference between disagreement or just that he was in the depths of thought, as I unfolded my convictions. When I was finished, after a few moments of reflection, he finally spoke.

"You have still left a lot of questions unanswered! And you must admit that your view still has a lot of problems!"

"Yes, sir, but what position doesn't leave a lot of questions? I don't know of any position on this subject that can answer all the problems and questions. It seems that some people leave one position because of a question or problem, and then quickly embrace another position without even realizing that the new position has as many questions as the old view, which was just jettisoned! And besides, the final question is not which view has the fewest number of problems or questions, but which view is the Biblical view, regardless of difficulties which may remain. I am sure you will agree that when we are studying theology and seeking to understand God and His ways, there will always be such questions, which will remain.

"Did we demand that all the questions must be answered before we embraced the doctrine of the Trinity---three persons in one Godhead? Did we do the same before we embraced the doctrine of the incarnation---Jesus is completely God and completely man? Can we answer all questions pertaining to those doctrines? Hardly! How then can we expect to answer all questions concerning God's sovereignty and man's will and responsibility before God?"

Chapter 9

Our time for study had expired, but not before Dr. Sisk made one last statement.

"I know God is sovereign, but I do admit that I have a problem with His sovereignty and the will of man---especially the wicked deeds performed by the wicked wills of wicked men. How could God ever have foreordained some of the despicable deeds of the most depraved and perverted men?"

With that our study came to a close. I prayed, asking God to guide us in our ability to understand that which we could understand, and to trust Him in areas which were beyond our ability to understand, noting that the secret things belong unto the Lord and the revealed things belong to us (Deuteronomy 29:29).

As we walked back across the campus, I told Dink, "Something very negative has taken place in Dr. Sisk's life, since I knew him years ago, which has stirred him deeply in his theology. I don't know what it is, but I know he is a different man. It may be twenty years later, but those years of walking with the Lord should not have made a man as sober and as uncertain in his theology, as he is now."

"Well, Preacha, I didn't know him back in dose days very well. He was still teachin' at da college when I got saved, but I never got as close ta him as you did. But I would agree wid ya dat he's a very sober an' somber fellow wid a lot on his mind, an' I don't think dat it's just da burden of da seminary!"

I didn't want to pry into Dr. Sisk's past life nor his business! But I did begin to pray that the Lord would bring to my attention what it was that had impacted him so deeply, that he became such a critic of Calvinism to the extent that he wanted to redefine his position, which was Arminian, and call it Calvinism.

It wasn't until a few weeks later that the Lord answered my prayer. I was preaching in an old friend's church, a friend from my college days, and the subject came up. The friend was Herby Hoskins, who was still as vibrant and as on fire for the Lord, as he had been in our college days (see *A Journey in Inspiration,* Richbarry Press, 1998). I decided to ask him if he knew anything of a difficult or tragic nature, which had taken place in Dr. Sisk's life, since the days we knew him back in our college days.

"You mean you don't know what he and his wife went through just a few years ago?'

"No, I lost track of him through the years? What happened and how serious was it?" I asked.

"Well, the way I understand it, his son was a brilliant kid, who came under the influence of some pretty wicked guy, when he went off to college to study science," he began. "As time passed, the son became more and more hardened towards the things of the Lord, and they tried to guide him back to his early Christian profession. But then one day he got mad at them and disowned them and their Christian faith, and they have never seen him since. They have spent all of their life savings just trying to find him, but there is no sign of him at all---anywhere!"

"That sure could explain Dr. Sisk's change of theology! Or at least his closed mind to Calvinism!" I asserted. "He must be wondering how God could have ever foreordained an action like that. He must be thinking that such a belief might make God the author of man's sin? Surely he has concluded that man called that shot concerning his son's actions---not God!"

"Yeah," Herby replied, "that's where the rubber of theology hits the road in a very practical way! How are you going to handle this one, Dr. Pointer?" he asked, with the emphasis on the word "Dr," as if my doctorate in theology should give me the answer.

"There is an answer!" I told him. "But the first question I must answer is how I am going to bring this subject up, or even better, how can I help him bring the subject to the floor of our discussions. I am sorry that he and his wife have had to go through this whole ordeal, and my heart truly goes out to them, but I would also not like to lose my job because of a theological question for which they think there is no answer. I will just trust the Lord, as always, to bring this question before us in one of our coming sessions. Or perhaps I can introduce the Biblical verses which answer the question, without specifically mentioning his particular trial and sorrow."

After I finished my preaching that day at Herby's church, I began thinking and praying about the matter, as I drove home. I wondered if Dink and I could help find the boy, and even do something to reunite him with his parents. But where would we begin? And would we not need the permission of the father and mother? Maybe I could run a preliminary search through my good friend, Mac Turnover, the owner of Turnover News Agency. Maybe I wouldn't need the permission of his parents to do that. So when I got home I called Mac and explained the situation to him. I gave him the son's name, Daryl Sisk, and told him about Dr. Sisk, and he said he would be glad to try to help us. But I told him also under no circumstances should he or anyone from his new agency contact the parents or the son, should the son be located.

This was just a preliminary search---so I thought!

Chapter 10

It was several days before I heard from Mac, and the news was not good. The report was that Daryl Sisk was dead! And this raised a series of further questions. Should we tell his parents? Were we positive he was dead? Could there have been a mistake? Could he still be alive? Shouldn't we verify the matter beyond any shadow of a doubt, before we even mentioned anything to his parents?

As Mac and I discussed it, we agreed that the story needed checking for its validity before we did anything else. The information Mac had turned up indicated that the boy had drowned in a lake accident in northern Minnesota a number of months ago. Mac offered to pay for our airline tickets, if Dink and I would fly up to Minnesota and meet him there on Friday evening. This would give us the weekend to investigate the accident and its supposed results. I didn't even have to ask Dink, as I knew he would go, so on Friday afternoon, we were off to Minnesota.

Since it was the fall, the leaves were far advanced in their colors compared to ours in the south, as was the temperature and its chill. Very beautiful weather, but somewhat cooler to a southern body of flesh and bones, whose blood was still thin from warmer weather. Mac had a local employee of his news organization meet us at the airport in Minneapolis-St. Paul, and then drive us several hours further north to the area, where the boy was supposed to have died. By the time we got there, and had checked into a motel and eaten supper with Mac, it was time to get to bed, so we could start early the next morning in our search for information.

While we ate, we decided on our plan for the next day. I would check the local newspapers for any information on the young man's death. Dink would go see the local police for any help they might be. Mac would go to the area of the accident and ask the natives what they had seen or heard about the whole matter. Perhaps someone knew something that could help us. After a night of rest and an early morning breakfast, we were off on our various paths of responsibility to see what we could find. We were to meet back at the motel about two o'clock for a late lunch and to discuss our different routes of inquiry.

When we were reunited, the conclusion was unanimous---the boy was really dead. Dink had found the police very helpful, and their information pointed undeniably to that conclusion. Mac had talked with a number of people, and their information reached the same conclusion. I had scanned all the newspapers from the supposed date of his death and the weeks following, and they too confirmed the reports of the others. Thus, all the data seemed to be in agreement that Daryl Sisk had died in a boating accident, while out on the lake late one night. His boat had exploded, and it was assumed that he had died in some manner, since no body had ever been found. Even if he had survived the explosion, the assumption was that he could never have swum to safety, because of the distance to the shore. So they believed he had drowned.

We spent a long time at the table even after we had finished our meal, discussing what we should do now. Did we feel confident that we had found the truth? Yes! Did we not have an obligation to present to the parents the evidence we had found? Yes! The only question now was, who should tell them? Me, or Dink or Mac?

Chapter 11

The trip home from Minnesota was not an easy one, especially since Dink and Mac had agreed that I was the one to tell Dr. Sisk and his wife about the death of their son. Therefore, my mind was searching for a when and a how to handle such a delicate matter. I decided at our next meeting I would share the sad news with Dr. Sisk, and then go with him, if he desired, to share it with his wife. I saw no way I could get them together to tell them without raising some suspicion.

Also on my mind was the subject of our next study. I decided that we would answer Dr. Sisk's concern that he had stated in our previous meeting, as he had said:

I know God is sovereign, but I do admit that I have a problem with His sovereignty and the will of man--- especially the wicked deeds performed by the wicked wills of wicked men. How could God ever have foreordained some of the despicable deeds of depraved and perverted men?

ACTS 2:23

We began our study with Acts 2:23, though we had mentioned this verse before, which says:

Him (Christ), being delivered by the determinate counsel and foreknowledge of God, ye have taken, and by wicked hands have crucified and slain.

that One (Christ) was delivered or surrendered over
(to the men mentioned in Acts 4:27-28)

> by the appointed decree
>> and by the previously determined counsel
>>> (or by the ordained will of God)
> you have taken and by lawless hands
>> have crucified and killed him

I explained the passage as I had before as follows:

Note---some would want to translate the first of the above phrases (the determinate counsel) to refer to God's appointed decree and the second one (foreknowledge) to refer to His foreknowing. Actually, the second word in the Greek, which is translated by many as "foreknowledge" can mean either foreknowledge or foreordination. Thus, we must look for some reason as to how we would translate it one way or the other. At this point I asked them to remember the Granville Sharp rule, which says that if we have an article (the) with a noun connected to another noun with the word "and" (Greek *kai*), it speaks of the same thing, if the second noun does not have the article. If it has the article with both nouns, then it is speaking of two different things. Therefore, we have translated the two words as referring to the same thing in different terms (appointed decree and previously determined counsel), rather than seeing them as referring to God's appointed decree in the first noun and to His foreknowledge in the second instance. Our conclusion is that the author is not speaking of foreordination here in the first word and foreknowing in the second noun, but of God's foreordination and decree in both words.

It would be our conclusion that in this passage we have the harmony of God's sovereignty and man's responsibility, something we must never confuse. God decrees and man acts responsibly, when he carries out God's decree and will. God decrees or foreordains something and human responsibility fulfills God's decree. This is clearly what the text says. But God is not the author of the sin of those who crucified Christ. God decreed Christ to be delivered to these wicked men, and when they crucified him they were fulfilling God's purpose and plan, or God never would have delivered Christ to them, but God was not the author of their sin.

I then asked if anything could happen to any of our children outside of the will and purpose of God? If God gave His own Son over to wicked men for crucifixion without committing sin Himself, and those wicked men carried out God's plan, then could not the same happen in our lives? But we must remember that God had a purpose in what He did in the death of His Son, for His Son's death brought about the salvation of a people. And would not our great omniscient God also have a purpose for the events in the lives of our loved ones---even that which was done by wicked men, even though we did not understand what He was doing? Is that not the hour that we must trust Him, and is not He the great omniscient and omnipotent and loving God, who is worthy of our trust, whatever comes into our lives, even if we do not understand the event?

ACTS 4:27-28

But our next verse is even clearer and undeniable in its message of our God's sovereignty over all things, even the wills of men, yea, the wicked wills of men.

Again I repeated Acts 4:27-28 and our considerations, as we had discussed it before:

For of a truth against thy holy child, Jesus, whom thou hast anointed, both Herod and Pontius Pilate, with the nations, and the people of Israel, were gathered together, to do whatever thy hand and thy counsel determined before to be done

This verse says very clearly that Herod and Pilate
along with the nations and people of Israel
were gathered together against Jesus
to do whatever God's hand and counsel
ordained before hand to be done
predetermined to come to pass
preordained to unfold in history
predestinated to be done

This makes God's sovereignty over the wicked acts of men even clearer. All those who were involved in the death of Christ, including Herod, and Pilate, and the nations and Israel, gathered together to do, yes, what they had willed to do. But their actions, as they performed them, were in accordance with God's predetermined counsel and will, yet they acted responsibly as they persecuted and crucified Christ. Again, we see the perfect harmony of God's determined will being carried out by men who were responsible for their actions and deeds, with God being sovereign over the totality of their actions in crucifying His own Son, and yet God not being the author of their sin.

We must conclude then that God is sovereign over all things, including men's actions, but men are responsible for all that they do by their sinful wills. It is not that God is sovereign simply to give men a free will to do what they want! But it is that men carry out the plan and purpose of God in what they do, and they are responsible for their actions, not God. This is clearly the teaching of Scripture.

Thus, once more, if God is sovereign over the deeds of wicked men, so is He sovereign over the actions of godly men. If God is sovereign over the actions of the men who crucified Christ, without violating their wills or forcing them or coercing them, then God is also sovereign over the actions of men when He saves them without violating or forcing or coercing their wills.

With that, Dink spoke up, and I think what he said almost knocked Dr. Sisk out of his chair.

"Preacha, can I say somethin' 'bout dis subject? I'se been tinkin' an' you'se tell me ifs I'm barkin' up da wrong tree here!"

I saw Dr. Sisk smile, as he looked down expecting, perhaps, some simple statement from a man for whom he evidently had little respect, just because he spoke with a little different nuance of the English language.

"I sees all dese people so concerned 'bout man's freedom! Dey tink dey must guard it so carefully, even ta da place wheres dey rob God of His sovereignty over all tings. Dats what dey do when dey says God is sovereign over all tings 'cept man's will! If dats so, and God ain't sovereign over man's will, den God ain't sovereign over all tings! A simple fellow like me tinks, wouldn't it be nice if men was as concerned 'bout protecten' God's sovereignty, as dey is 'bout protecten' man's freedom of da will?

"An' den I hears dem conclude dat if we say man doesn't have a totally free will, den we has dehumanized man! But wouldn't it be nice if men was as concerned 'bout de-deifying da God of heaven, when dey denys His sovereignty over all tings, as dey are 'bout de-humanizing poor little puny sinful man? Men tink deys got ta uphold man's great power of da will in salvation at all costs, even at da cost of denyin' da sovereignty of God! God becomes a little puppet reactin' ta man, if and when man decides ta believe, cause God doesn't have any control over da actions or will of man, so dey says!

"But den, I haves ta ask, if God is not sovereign over man's will in salvation, because dat would dehumanize man, den God would also dehumanize man, it seems ta me accordin' ta dem, if God was sovereign over man in any other area. Dat means dat God cannot be sovereign over man in any area, lest man is dehumanized. God can only react in every situation of life, accordin' ta man's will, cause man's will is totally free, an' anyting else would dehumanize man! But if one says dat man is free in one area, den he is free in every area, lest he be de-humanized, an' dat means dat God is shut out from His sovereignty over any thing pertainin' ta man!

"It seems ta me dat it's better ta understand it likes da Bible does in dose Acts verses, as we saw da preacha's explanation! God is absolutely sovereign an' man is fully responsible, which seems ta us like a contradiction. But why's can't we'se call it a mystery like da Trinity or da incarnation?"

Following a few moments of silence, Dr. Sisk could only say, "You have certainly given me a lot to think about today!"

Chapter 12

I asked Dr. Sisk if I could talk to him for a few minutes, after we had closed our discussion with prayer, and he agreed. I am sure he had no idea what our conversation would include, and I had little thought of how to begin to give him the bad news of the hour.

"Dr. Sisk, I have come across some information about your son, that I feel I must share with you."

I looked for some reaction, but didn't get much, or at least, as much as I thought I might.

"It has been verified with great certainty that your son is no longer alive!" I finally blurted out.

Again, he sat rather emotionless and unresponsive, and then he finally said, "Well, I had expected that! But he was already as good as dead to us! Nevertheless, can you give me the details?"

I went on to explain his son's demise in a boating accident in Minnesota, and that Dink and I and Mac Turnover of Turnover News Agency had been to Minnesota and interviewed the police, scoured the newspaper records, and talked to many others about the matter. I told him that they all had concluded that he had drowned following an explosion on the boat, and his body was never found.

He again sat motionless as I gave him these details, and he finally said, "Well, that ends not only the sad chapters of the past several years, but also the entire book of a sad life for him and for us. Now we can close the book and get on with our lives."

I asked him if he wanted me to go with him and explain the matter to his wife, and he assured me that there was no need for that. He would tell her and her reaction would be pretty much the same as his, as she would be as glad to close the book as he was on this sad event.

Then he added, "I will also share with her what we have studied this morning, the verses and the conclusions. I will assure her that God is sovereign in these matters, concerning our son, even though those involved, whatever the circumstances, were responsible for their deeds and actions. Oh, how we want at a time like this to be omniscient and know all the whys and wherefores of God's will and way. But we must be satisfied to know one thing, and that is that there are many secret things that belong unto the Lord---things we may understand someday, but not now, it seems, no matter how hard we try to scrutinize all these events in our minds. How easy it is to run the risk of coming to the wrong conclusions about a matter and in some manner denigrate God in His person and attributes in the process. This only adds greater sorrow to our lives!"

After we had prayed we parted, but not without one final observation from him, as he said, "That fellow Dink surprises you, doesn't he? And what a humble spirit he has in the process! No wonder so many seem drawn to him on this campus! He is just who he is, and he doesn't seem to care what anyone might think or say about him!"

As I walked back to my office, I couldn't help but wonder how all of this would play out in the matter of our future at the seminary. It was not that I was campaigning to stay, if the Lord didn't want me there. But perhaps we were making some headway with Dr. Sisk, by allowing him to see our approach to theology. It was not our sole concern to win some theological debate over theological issues, which had no application to everyday life. But to us theology is very practical, and the doctrine of the sovereignty of God is central to our theology and our lives!

Chapter 13

I was unusually tired, when I finally arrived home that night. I concluded it must have been for several reasons. First, it had been a whirlwind weekend, and secondly, a burden seemed to have been lifted, or at least there seemed to be a lifting of some of the pressure on Dink and me in the school situation. Maybe we had turned the corner in our discussions with Dr. Sisk, although I did wonder if one could conclude anything from what he said in light of the uncertainty of the sad news he had received at the end of our study. If he really was mellowing in his stance on Calvinism, maybe it might affect our future status.

I had barely slipped into my reclining chair in the family room, when Ira, Jr. came to me with a question. He was a freshman in college now, and we had spent many hours, as he grew up, discussing theology, and he always wanted to learn more. He wanted to know about the discussion time with Dr. Sisk. I filled him in a little on our meetings, and then he hit me with another question.

"Dad, I wondered if I could have a copy of your notes? There are several guys at my Christian college who want to study God's sovereignty together at lunch, and I thought this would be a good place to start---the sovereignty of God and the will of man!"

"Do they know any theology?" I asked. "This would be a difficult place to begin with someone, if they were ill-prepared for the subject!"

"Well, Dad, in our Christian high school, most of us studied the subject some in our classes, but not in any depth, and we have been discussing it at lunch. We seem to be a pretty objective group---they want to study it just so they can understand it. So I don't think anyone is going to get all bent out of shape over it---at least I hope not!"

"Then I will make you copies of it on one condition --- that if anyone starts to get uptight over the subject, you will immediately discontinue your study!" I declared.

He had no problem agreeing with that, and so I went upstairs to my study and made him several copies of my notes which I had prepared thus far. I told him, as I gave them to him, that since I was several weeks ahead on the studies, the notes would be ready for him as he needed them week by week. This suited him fine, he said, as they were going to meet weekly, also.

Then he smiled as he said, "And April and I want to study them together on Saturday nights, when I go to visit her!" I could have guessed that. He was speaking of April Showers, a young lady about his age, who he had known from childhood! (See *A Journey in Salvation*, Richbarry Press, 2001) He went to see her every Saturday night, even though she lived an hour or more away, and both sets of parents felt it best that they be just friends during this time of their lives. They enjoyed each other's company, especially learning the truth of God's Word together. Shades of the good old days, when his mother and I were dating, prior to our marriage! (See *A Journey in Grace,* Richbarry Press, 1990)

The week and weekend passed swiftly, and I was eager for Monday, but hesitant, as I knew I would see Dr. Sisk early in the week for our discussion time. I didn't want to appear too nosy about his wife's reaction to the news of her son's death, but on the other hand, I didn't want to be seen as uncaring and say nothing, if he wanted to talk about it.

Understandably, it was with some anxiety that I waited the arrival of our next discussion hour!

Chapter 14

I was a little uneasy and uncertain, as Dink and I made our way to Dr. Sisk's office that morning for our study of God's sovereignty. I tried to read his mood, as always, but at the best of times that was not easy, let alone in a time of difficulty.   After the normal greetings, from which I received no help in my analysis, I decided to press on in the matter of the subject before us. I had decided to review the previous material with some expansion, in that it is always helpful for teachers and preachers to summarize and review at key points of a study or a sermon. How easy it is for students or a congregation to get lost in the forest, rather than being able to see the overall progress of thought as the subject unfolds. I summarized the previous material as follows, and that became our basis of discussion for the day.

1. God is sovereign over all things!

    This statement means exactly what it says. God is sovereign over every event, including man and all of God's creatures and creation in all their actions. To say anything else leaves God as merely a reactionary to the sovereign actions of someone or something else, who or which is not under His will and control.   Then the question becomes, who is the one who is sovereign in these situations, if God is not? Man or even the devil?

    If man was sovereign over even one event of his own life, would that not unleash a series of events over which God was not sovereign, which series of events would be multiplied again and again? Would that not result in a continual spiraling of further events, whereby God would become less and less sovereign as history unfolded?

And would that not also be true if Satan, the great enemy of God, were sovereign over even one event? Would not the following events, which multiplied from that one action, bring a greater and greater loss of the sovereignty of God as history unfolded?

And would that not remove man more and more out from under the sovereign control of God's power, and would it not be the same for Satan? Or would we allow man and Satan one action or some actions out from under God's sovereignty, and then all the other events we would claim were back under God's sovereign will?

The crux of the matter is that there cannot be two sovereigns. The moment we speak of God not being sovereign over one thing, He ceases to be sovereign period! Even if we say that in His sovereignty He gave man a totally free will in the matter of salvation, is that not to say that God is not sovereign over the work of salvation, as salvation is left up to the determination of man's will? One cannot have God and man both as sovereigns. One cannot say God in His sovereignty decided not to be sovereign at one point of His sovereignty, and yet claim He is still sovereign.

The question is very clear here! Where does the Bible teach any of the above attempts to make both man and God sovereign? If God is not sovereign over all events and actions, then someone else is sovereign over all events and actions or some events and actions. What a frightening thought that should be to every clear thinking Christian!

2. The will of man is not sovereign over any event, but yet man acts freely and is a responsible being in all his actions!

    Initially, this might sound a little frightening and confusing as well! I can almost hear the cries of fatalism, or that such would make man nothing but a robot or an automaton, or don't forget whosoever will, as if man's will is totally free in all events and actions. Yet, must we not admit that man's will is free in one sense, but not in another?

    In his natural and physical being man is not free in all things. Man is bound and restricted by his physical nature in many things. Man cannot fly like a bird by flapping his arms as much as he might want to fly and even try to fly, because he is limited and restricted in his physical make up and being. Man cannot will to know something, which is beyond his being. Man cannot will to be something that is beyond his nature. He cannot will to be omnipotent or omniscient or omnipresent---he is limited in his nature! We must admit that man's will is not free in matters pertaining to his physical being and physical nature. He is only free to do that which is possible within the confines of his human ability.

    But is not the same true when it comes to man's spiritual being? Man is a sinner by nature, since the fall of Adam. He cannot will anything, which is not possible within the context of his nature of sin. He possesses a blind mind, an enslaved will, and affections, which are no longer capable of being turned to God in man's own strength. His nature of sin limits him in his mind, in his will and in his affections. As much as man might will to save himself by his own works, and as many works as he might do over a period of years or decades, there is no way he can ever do enough good works to save himself. The Bible makes it clear that man is incapable of such good works, no matter how hard his will might want or claim or try.

Is not Paul clear in what he says in Romans 3?

> 10 There is none righteous---no, not one!
> 11 There is none that understandeth!
> 12 There is none that seeketh after God!
> 12 They are all gone out of the way!
> 12 They are together become unprofitable!
> 18 There is no fear of God before their eyes!

Thus, man is free do that which he is able to do within the confines of his sinful nature. But he is not free to do any thing outside of the context of his nature of sin, which includes the exercise of his own will in his own strength and power, whereby he is able to be saved! This is why the Bible says that salvation is of the Lord! This is what is called monergism---salvation is the work of God alone! We are saved by the power and grace of God alone. Faith is even the gift of God! Synergism is the doctrine of the Roman Catholic Church and of Arminian theology, which says that salvation is by the cooperation of God and man. God gives an initial grace (prevenient grace), and man is saved IF he decides to respond to this initial giving of grace by God.

I had hoped to take another step in my outline, but because we stopped and discussed the above material as we went through it, our hour was soon gone. The key question raised by Dr. Sisk was the one I had anticipated, and which the next section of our material covered, but which we did not have the time to discuss today. What about the will of man? If God is sovereign even over the will of man, how can God hold man accountable for his sin? Does this not make God the author of man's sin? What about the responsibility of man to repent and believe the gospel?

One thing was certain---there cannot be two sovereigns. God is the sovereign One, and man is not sovereign. But man is still responsible for his actions and his sin! But how do we explain this? And is this Scriptural?

As we closed and Dink and I left Dr. Sisk's office, I was sorry that he had not said anything to me about his son and his wife's reaction to the news of his death. I wondered if he knew how much we wanted to help them and minister to them at this time. How he had changed since I had known him those years ago in college!

Chapter 15

How surprised I was as Dink and I left Dr. Sisk's office, when he literally came running after me and called me back, after I was halfway down the hall. Dink went on, not that he wouldn't have come back with me, but he wasn't certain he was included in the invitation to return. Dr. Sisk asked me to sit down, and with a strained look on his face he shocked me with the latest concerning his son.

"When I got home, my wife said Daryl had called her that very day, and that clearly he was still alive. He even told her, supposedly, not to believe any reports of his death. They would all be false!" Dr. Sisk told me.

"Did he mention any reason why the reports would be false?" I asked. "Did he mention the boat accident to her, whereby he was supposed to have been killed? Is there any doubt in your mind about the reliability of her story, in light of what she has been through these past several months? Could she be delusional, or just making up the story for some other reason?"

"No, he didn't say anything else about the reports. But to be honest with you, I can't be absolutely positive that she is telling the truth about a phone call from him. It could be the strong desire she has not to believe the story of his death. She did evidence that when I told her Friday. She said she would not believe the report, until she saw the body!" he said, as he answered my questions.

"Did he say where he was now?" was my next question.

"No, she said she asked him, but he wouldn't tell her. He said he still had a lot of things to work out before he would ever come home, but urged her not to worry about him. He said he was trying to work things out, but that he was still struggling."

"So what are you going to do now?" I asked again.

"What can I do but wait? I thought you and Dink might have some ideas," he said hopefully.

I wished I could have told him, yes, we can try this, this and this! But to be honest with him, at the moment I saw nothing we could do. There were too many unanswered questions concerning the whole issue. First, was he really still alive? Second, if alive, was he still in Minnesota? Third, could we ever find him, even if we were positive he was still alive in Minnesota? One could spend a lot of time, money and effort trying to find answers to any one of those questions, and still come away empty. We seemed stymied once again!

It was with a large measure of sadness that I left Dr. Sisk's office. I took with me a picture of his son, Daryl. I didn't remember ever having met the boy, so I wanted one for future reference, and I thought I might send it to Mac Turnover. I even took it home with me and put it on the desk in my study.

What a shock when Ira, Jr., came in and after seeing it there asked, "Hey, where'd you get Randal's picture?"

"Randal?" I asked. "You know this guy as Randal?"

"Well, sure, Dad! He's one of the guys in our group that is studying sovereignty, but I don't think he is saved! How do you know him?" he asked somewhat bewildered.

"He doesn't know me! But I know of him! This is Dr. Sisk's son---the boy who was supposedly killed in a boat accident in Minnesota! He's in your study group and living in this town---now?" I asked with great interest.

Chapter 16

Ira, Jr., informed me that Daryl was living in Seminary City, and he worked evenings, while going to school in the daytime. What a surprise to learn he was going to the same local Christian college that Ira was attending. This meant that he was living right under his parents' nose.

"Well, isn't he afraid that he might run into his parents somewhere out and about here in Seminary City?" I queried.

"Oh, he doesn't get out much, I would guess, and maybe he knows all the places his parents would frequent, and so he stays away from them. That would be my guess. I think I could do the same, if I ever decided to do what he is doing!" he informed me with a sneaky smile.

I returned the smile and said, "You might be able to do that, but when your mother and I got hold of you again, you would be very sorry!"

"Yes, that's why I would never do any such thing as stupid as that!" he politely informed me with a return smile.

When Ira, Jr., had left the room, I pondered the problem I was facing. Do I go by myself and talk to the boy, or do I send young Ira to tell him I want to see him? Do I inform his father where he is, or would that sour the boy all the more against not only his parents, but also against young Ira and me? Or do I send Dink to talk to him? He had never met Dink, and Dink could plan to meet him casually, and then get to know him, and offer to help him without scaring him off. Dink had a way about him whereby he could befriend him without arousing his suspicions. But what if that backfired, and the boy took off again, and his parents learned of it? That surely would leave a bad taste in their mouths concerning Dink and me, which might even seal the question of our future at the seminary.

I decided that we could not think of ourselves, but had to consider what was best for this young man. Obviously, he did not want to see his parents at this time, so bringing them in on it, as much as they would want to be included, was out of the question. We would just have to trust the Lord in the matter, and let the chips sovereignly fall where He willed, even if it cost us our positions at the seminary! Dink was the man for the job. So I called him and filled him in on the whole situation. As usual, he never was at a loss for a comment or two.

"Preacha, wish I was as sure 'bout dis as you are in tinkin' dat I'm da man ta go see da boy! But if you'se tinks so, I'll give it a shot!"

So in his spare time, Dink began to shadow the boy, just to get a pattern of his life and whereabouts during certain times of the day. That way he could know what would be the best time and place to see if they could have an unexpected and unplanned meeting (from the boy's perspective). Once the contact was established, and Dink had gained his confidence, he would tell him who he was, and assure him that his presence in the city and his place of dwelling were confidential matters.

Things went as planned, and within several days Dink had a place where he thought it would be best to meet him. Randal (or Daryl) always ate breakfast at a certain fast food place at a certain early hour of the day, even sitting in a certain booth to read the morning paper for about thirty minutes. He never varied, so Dink was there one day earlier than Daryl normally arrived, so that when he did come in, his usual booth was already taken by Dink. We were banking on the fact that creatures of habit are not happy when their habit is broken, and sure enough, when Daryl found Dink in his booth, he said nothing the first day. On the second day, it was too much for him. He was very polite, but he had to ask Dink if he was going to eat breakfast here at this fast food place every day. I was witness to all of this, as I was seated in a booth nearby, so I could see and hear the entire conversation.

Dink smiled, and offered him the other seat in that booth, and they both sat there reading their papers and eating, neither one saying a word. After several days they struck up a conversation, and a friendship was born! After all, what did Daryl have to fear from a guy as friendly as Dink, who seemed to be so simple and uncomplicated, alongside most of the people he had known in his life. And, furthermore, what harm could come to him from a fellow who butchered the English language in such a humorous and humble manner. Dink also seemed to provide Daryl a friend, something he needed so much just now.

Finally, after a number of days of casual conversation, Daryl opened up, as he said, "Dink, can I ask you a question?"

"Sure! Fire away! Anyting ya wants!" Dink answered. "I cain't guarantee no answers, but glad ta help ya!"

"Did you ever wonder about your parents?" he asked.

"Sure!" Dink answered. "I wondered if dey loved me! I wondered if I could ever measure up ta what dey wanted me ta be! I wondered why I jus' didn't leave home---it probably wouldn't make no difference ta dem, any how!"

"So what did you do?" Daryl asked, as Dink now had him hooked, but it was with the truth.

"I left home an' ran off an' joined a gang, which led ta a life in a mob called da Almandine. Not a very smart ting ta do! I was goin' no wheres fast in da wrong direction wid my life upside down till sometin' drastic happened!"

Dink had him hooked now, as he paused to let Daryl ask, "What happened?"

"Nuttin'! I didn't do a ting. It's what God did!" he said, and then paused to get another reaction from Daryl.

"What do you mean, it's what God did?" as Daryl asked the anticipated question.

"Yeah, it's what God did! You know---He saves ya. Ain't ya never been saved? Jesus does it! He comes an' changes yer life. It's called da new birth. He broke me down good, showed me what a sinner I was. Den He cleansed me from all my sins, an' gave me a new life! Can't beat dat, can ya?" Dink stated with a joyful lilt in his voice, which had to stir Daryl's heart!

Daryl sat there a few moments speechless, and then he asked, "But what about your parents? Didn't you have a real reason to leave home and stay gone? What did Jesus do about that?" Daryl asked almost sarcastically.

Dink countered with a chuckle, "I found out dey wasn't my problem---I was. I has ta admit dey weren't perfect parents, but in my sinful state I blamed dem fer all my problems, when I was really da fall guy. When I went back home, an' told dem what had happened, dey broke down an' cried an' told me how sorry dey was fer da way tings had been fer me. I told dem, it wasn't der fault---it was mine. I was just a stubborn, hard-heated, young, pigheaded, numbskull of a kid, an' I had nothin' 'gainst dem. Jesus had taken away all my hate an' rebellion."

"Do you see them now?" Daryl asked.

"Sure, an' dey just loves my wife. We has a great time now. An' deys even been saved by Jesus, too!"

I was about ready to cry, because all he said was true!

Chapter 17

While Dink and I waited for a break in his meetings with Daryl Sisk, we also had to keep our appointments for study with his father, even though it was getting close to the Christmas season. We weren't going to press Daryl, but let him determine when it was time to take each step. Dink had gained his confidence, and the whole situation was progressing, but it was slow. Patience was absolutely necessary. But then, we always wondered if time was a factor? Would he decide to leave town once again? Or could he find out who we were, and if that happened, no one could predict what might be the result!

Obviously, it was with some difficulty that Dink and I met with Dr. Sisk for our next session of study. We both were ready to overflow in our joy that we knew his son was alive and even in Seminary City. But we felt we could not divulge that information, due to the fact that we thought Daryl's parents might run right to him, and that could cause him to flee the city from us, his parents, and even cause him to go into hiding once again. So we muffled our joy, as we met to discuss God's sovereignty.

I began by giving the first two thoughts of our study, which also included some expansion of our subject with further comments. We had dealt with two points. The first said that God is sovereign over all things, and the first part of the second point said that the will of man is not sovereign over any event, yet man acts freely. Now we were ready to discuss the fact that man is a responsible being in all his actions. I restated clearly our first two thoughts:

1. God is sovereign over all things!

2. The will of man is not sovereign over any event, yet
   man acts freely and is a responsible being in all his
   actions!

I had to admit that this was a very difficult subject.
Surely, it is proper to ask how God could be sovereign over
all things, and yet man acts freely with responsibility for all
of his actions. It would seem to our human reasoning that
if God was sovereign over all things, man could not act
freely in any matter, nor could he be a responsible being for
any of his actions.

But we had already discussed two passages (Acts 2:23
and Acts 4:27-28), which showed very clearly that sinful
men, acting freely doing evil deeds, were fulfilling the will
of God, as they crucified Jesus Christ, the Son of God. So
the question we faced now was, does this not make God the
author of their sin, and relieve them of all responsibility for
their actions?

I decided that we would look at Romans 9, where Paul
defines and then defends his doctrine of election, and in the
process answers these questions very clearly.

In Romans 9-11 Paul is answering an apparent problem
that he knew his discussion of justification by faith would
bring to the minds of the Jews of his day. He had just set
forth clearly and undeniably a doctrine of salvation
(justification by faith), which would exclude the multitudes
of his fellow Jews from the covenant of God---something,
which was unthinkable to the Jews of his day. They had
built a massive but erroneous system of salvation by works
through the keeping of the law. Now Paul comes along and
tells them in the earlier chapters of Romans that they are
not saved by keeping the law, but by faith alone. Thus,
there comes the question: what about the Jews? What

about the covenant which God made with the Jews, according to Paul's view of justification by faith alone?

Though Paul had set forth in the second chapter of Romans his answer to that question, he now understands that he must explain the matter once more. In Romans 2 he had said that one is not a Jew just because he is a member of the Jewish race, that is, national Israel. But a true Jew is one who knows God by faith in His Son, Jesus Christ. It is possible, therefore, to be a Jew by nationality, but not a true Jew spiritually, according to Paul

Then, having discussed in fullness his doctrine of justification by faith alone in the intervening chapters of Romans, the question comes with even greater force---what about the Jews? Paul's view of salvation by faith, as the Jews of his day saw it, meant that God was not keeping His covenant promise with His chosen people. Paul must explain to them once again in greater detail how God is keeping His covenant, when so many of national Israel would be ruled out by Paul's doctrine of salvation.

Therefore, in Romans 9:1-13 Paul gives us his view of election as the basis of God's salvation!

I   THE PROPER DEFINITION OF ELECTION   1-13

A. The true Israel is denunciated Scripturally! 1-8

1.   *The true Israel is not fleshly Israel   1-5*

Paul is burdened for Israel of the flesh   1-3
let no one deny that

Paul recognizes the Israel of the flesh   4-5
   but as much respect as he has
     for the nation of Israel
      they are not the true Israel

2. *The true Israel is the spiritual Israel   6-8*

the Word of God had not failed   6
   because of the unbelief of fleshly Israel
the Word of God is fulfilled   7-8
   not in fleshly Israel
     but in the spiritual Israel---
      that is in the seed of Isaac---
       Jews and Gentiles---
        that is in those born
         supernaturally of God

B. The true Israel is entered sovereignly!   9-13

1. *The basis of election is clearly stated   9-11*

Isaac is an example of one born   9-10
   by the power of God alone---
     a supernatural birth physically---
      which is symbolic of salvation
       in that any one who is saved has
        a supernatural birth spiritually
Jacob is an example also of one who is   11-13
   a true heir by the will of God alone
     and not in accordance with the ways
     and will of any man

I was surprised that our study of these first thirteen verses took all of our study time, and we didn't have the opportunity to finish the rest of the chapter as planned. But I was glad that we did get to nail down several points, with which we all seemed to agree.

1. We had identified the true Israel of God---chosen Jews and chosen Gentiles!

2, These Jews and Gentiles, the true Israel of God, had been elected by God!

3. It was on this basis of election that they had been given new life by the power of God!

As we ended our time of study, Dr. Sisk asked a question that I hoped I would never have to face.

"If you men ever know the truth of my son being alive and his whereabouts, you would tell us, wouldn't you?"

My first thought concerned where he got such an idea? Was it information from someone else? Or was it that he did not trust us? Or was he simply checking to see if he could trust us for sure? But how could he possibly have gotten any information on this matter? Though his son lived in the city, the family was new in the city and they knew very few people. It was not that the boy had grown up in Seminary City, and had a lot of friends here, or that his parents had a lot of friends here, also. There had never been a time, when he was with his parents in this city, even when they were introduced to the seminary family, as the new president and his wife.

But I still had to wonder if he knew Daryl was in our very city!

Chapter 18

When Dr. Sisk asked that question, would we tell him if we knew his son Daryl was alive and in our city, I looked at Dink and he looked at me. I feared Dr. Sisk could read our minds, just by our looks.

But then quickly I asked him a question. "Dr. Sisk, do you want us to make you a promise that we might someday have to break?"

He was quick to fire back, "What do you mean by that? How could that ever be! I would expect you to tell me whatever you knew about my own son!"

He said it with force and strength and conviction, not leaving any open door for us not to tell him. So I asked him, "What if the time would come, when our telling you would possibly hurt him and drive him away from you even further and maybe forever? What if he did not want you to know? What if he was working through some things, with which he was not finished, and needed more time before he wanted to see you? What if he was still confused and uncertain? Would you want someone to tell you where he was, so that you or your wife would immediately run to find him? Could you stop your wife from seeking to find him, if she knew he was alive and where he was?"

"Are you telling me that you know he is alive and where he is?" he asked bluntly, still very upset.

"No, I am not telling you anything, except what I just said!" I stated emphatically, not lying to him, but restating my conviction.

"Well, if I find out that you know now or you find out later where he is, and you didn't tell me, I can assure you, there is no doubt about our relationship with one another!" he declared, making rather clear what he meant in no uncertain terms. Dink and I both took it to mean that would be the end of our days at this school.

"Dr. Sisk, I wish I could tell you your son was alive and where he was, but I cannot!" I stated in less than certain words, not to deceive, but to protect the son from his parents, maybe due to no wrong on their part, but because something was wrong with the son and his attitude towards them, whatever the reason.

As we left the room, Dr. Sisk said, "Just remember my words! I have a right to know about my own son!"

Then, when Dink and I were walking back to our offices, Dink said, "Preacha, ya sure danced around dat one like some silver-slippered professional! Does ya tink he believes his son is alive, and we'se knows it, or dat you was just speakin' in general terms?"

"Well, whatever he might think," I explained, "we both know that it would be a disaster if we told them about their son, and they ran to find him before he is ready to see them. We would lose his trust, and they would lose a son, maybe forever! You keep working with him, Dink, and eventually the real reason for his bitterness with his parents will come to the surface."

When I got back to my office, I stretched out on my couch for a few minutes to contemplate what it could be that bothered Daryl so much about his relationship with his parents. Was it his problem or was it theirs? If it was the parents' fault, was it one parent who was at fault or both of them? If one, which one, and why?

As I thought, I had to conclude that we had done the right thing. A young man's life could be hanging in the balance!

Chapter 19

Dink's meetings with Daryl continued to go well, as the boy opened up more and more in the friendship with him. But then one day, it all appeared to go sour, as Daryl walked in and began to question Dink immediately. He didn't even have his newspaper, nor did he take time to buy breakfast. He made a beeline towards the booth where Dink was sitting.

"So, I understand you teach at the seminary!" he exclaimed with some rage.

But Dink didn't even look up from his paper as he answered, "Yeah! So what? Does dat trouble ya?"

"Yes, it does, and you should know why, especially if you are a spy sent by my father!" he said with some fury, yet knowing enough to keep his voice as soft as possible.

"Look, ifs I had been sent by yer parents, an' dey knew we was meetin' fer breakfast ever' morning, dontcha tink dey would have been here by now to see ya an' ta talk ta ya? Calm down an' go getcha some breakfast on me, an' we'se can talk 'bout it!" Dink said as he tried to hand him a five dollar bill.

"I don't need your help, and I don't need your money!" he declared, and turned and walked away.

I must admit that I wondered, as Dink probably did also, whether he might be going to buy his breakfast, so he could return to the table, or if he was going to walk right out the door and disappear once again, even leaving town! I guess we shouldn't have been surprised, when he kept on walking out the door! But still it hurt! Only God knew if we would ever see him again!

Our hearts were still heavy, when a few hours later we met with Dr. Sisk. We had decided to continue our silence about his son, hoping perhaps the boy might come back to meet with Dink the next morning or so. We would be there for sure, even for a week or more, not breaking our previous pattern, just in case the boy did have a change of heart, or if he came by just to see if Dink was there.

Several hours later, even though it was Christmas week, we were in Dr. Sisk's office, and after some words of greeting, we plunged into our subject, and nothing was said about the son, for which we were grateful!

I began and continued our study from Romans 9:14-23 (with their reactions from time to time, which are not included here) as follows:

Introduction

1. A brief review

    In our previous study Paul gave his definition of sovereign election in salvation. But he also saw clearly that there would always be certain objections to such a view. Therefore, he now turns to defend his position of sovereign grace in election against possible objections.

2. One further important point

    But before moving into Paul's defense of the sovereign election of a people by God, we must take note of one very important point. The objections that Paul anticipates would never have come, if Paul had presented any other view of election, besides an election based on the sovereign will and sovereign grace of God. Who would object, if Paul were teaching an Arminian view (or what some might call falsely a modified Calvinistic view), which puts the final choice in election in some manner in the hands of man and his ability to choose God in his own strength or power or even by prevenient grace? The objections we see Paul anticipating are absolutely unnecessary and irrelevant, unless Paul is teaching salvation by the sovereign grace of God.

3. The objections recognized

One can almost picture Paul presenting his view, and then an Israelite, who had been listening saying, "Election by the will of God alone and not by the law or the works of man? And all according to God's will? Wait a minute, Paul! Your view has a lot of problems and raises a lot of questions! Let me state them for you, and you give me the answers, if you can!"

Which one of us, who previously denied salvation by the sovereign grace of God and felt we had to give man some ability of his own in the matter of response to God first before God would save us by His power, ever heard the objections we will see now? We heard no such objections, when we were promoting a synergistic view of salvation. But the first time we presented the Biblical monergistic view (God alone), we heard the following objections immediately! Thus, the reality and clarity of the objections give clear evidence that we have interpreted Paul correctly in the previous verses, as he presented his view of sovereign grace in salvation.

II   THE POWERFUL DEFENSE OF ELECTION 9:14-23

A. Objection One

1. *Stated 14*

What shall we say? Is there unrighteousness with God?

Paul, your view of election
    makes God unrighteous
    makes God unfair
Paul, is it not unfair of God
    to choose one over another
        based on His will
           and His will alone with no part
              of His choice based on man---
              man's will
              man's works
              man's desire
Paul, I just cannot believe a view like that!!!

2. *Objection One Answered 15-18*

verse 14
    God forbid such a thought
        that would accuse God of being unfair
           or unrighteous
    absolutely not!
    that cannot be!

verses 15-16
    God is sovereign in His mercy and grace

Have you never read in the OT Scripture
(see Exodus 33:19)
where God says   15
I will have mercy on whom
I will have mercy
I will exercise grace towards
whomever I wish
to show grace
do you not see that salvation   16
is not of the one willing---
by human choice
is not by running---
that is by running
a certain course
of conduct---
or by human works
but salvation is of God---
the One who shows mercy---
and remember verse 15---
God shows mercy and grace
on whom He wishes/wills
verse 17
Do you not see the other side of this truth?
that God said to Pharaoh---Ex. 9:16
I raised you up into existence
I brought you on the stage of history
for this specific hour and purpose
I raised you up for two purposes
so that I might display my power in you
so that my name might be published
in all the earth

verse 18
> the conclusion of the matter is clear
>> God has mercy on whom He wills
>> God hardens whom He wills also
> a comment on these statements
>> Both are to be seen as by God's will and sovereignty---showing mercy on one and the hardening of another. If one wants to say, "But Pharaoh hardened his heart first," it must be noted that Paul ignores that consideration.   If that objection answers the problem Paul is dealing with here, then his whole previous discussion is superfluous and unnecessary.

The conclusion is clear! Paul's view of sovereign grace in election does not make God unfair!

B. Objection Two   19-23

 1. *The Objection Stated   19*

> *Then wilt thou say unto me, Why doth He yet find fault? For who has resisted His will?*

we can expand Paul's anticipated objection
> Paul, you say
>> that God wills to harden men?
>> that God puts that will in effect?
> then, Paul, I have some questions for you!
> why does God find fault with men
>> in what they do when they sin
>>> when they are not capable
>>>> of doing anything else?

how can God hold such a man accountable?
how can God condemn a man for sinning?
is not God the one who is responsible
    for a man's sin and inability to respond
        to God and His mercy and grace?
is not a man when he sins only carrying out
    the divine will and decree of God?
can God possibly find fault with a man
    if he is only carrying out God's decree?
I've got you now, Paul!
Surely, you've gone too far!!!

Again, note that the reader must admit that these objections are in order, only if Paul is teaching sovereign grace in salvation.

2. *Paul's Answer   20*

    a. A bold statement   20

Nay but O man, who are you that replies against God?

the objector is reminded of his humanity
    and God's person as Paul answers---
        Oh man---little puny man
        Who are YOU---emphatic use
        That YOU would reply against God!
        That YOU would be disputing God!
        That YOU would contradict God!
        That YOU would argue with God!
        That YOU would be judging God!

> the objector is reminded with Whom
> he is in dispute---
> WITH GOD!!!

Clearly, Paul doesn't really give an answer, but he gives a rebuke! Men must recognize that there comes a time when God has spoken, and little puny man must sit down and shut up, realizing that he is seeking to argue with God---the final and absolute authority over all things. When God has spoken, man cannot question God, but rather he must believe what God says. God does not have to explain His ways to man. And surely God's wisdom and knowledge of all things is so far above man, that man could never understand all things were God to explain them to him. Thus, God is God and man is the creature, and man does not have the right to demand all answers to God's will and ways. There is a limit to man's knowledge, and man must be satisfied with what God says, even though he cannot always understand the work and will of God.

For man to desire to go beyond his human limitations and God's boundaries is rebellion of the worst sort. Perhaps we could paraphrase Paul's answer here as follows, "Sit down and shut up, for you are in the presence of God, demanding to know and understand things, which you are not meant nor able to know and explain. Humble yourself before Him, for you are not arguing with or questioning a man, but you are arguing with and even questioning God in His wisdom and ways." This is not to say it is wrong to ask questions of God. But surely there is a right way and a wrong way to address the holy God of heaven with our questions. We must always acknowledge that because He is God, He may not answer us, when and how we so desire, as in the case of Job!

b. A convincing illustration

this does not seem to be a reference
as some might say to Jeremiah's
speaking of a potter
Paul raises a series of questions here

1) Will a vessel say to the potter, Why have
you made me this way?   20

Answer---No!

2) Does not the potter have power over the
clay to make one a valuable vessel and
another a worthless vessel?   21

Answer---Yes

3) What if God the potter wishes to make
and do with His vessels as He wills?   22

Answer---So what! He is God---He can
do as he pleases, and no one can
question Him.

4) What if God wishes to display His wrath
and power by bearing a vessel, which
has been prepared for destruction?

two possibilities in the original language
middle voice
a vessel which has prepared itself
for destruction

passive voice
a vessel which has been prepared
for destruction---the word
can mean "foreordained"
the context clearly pushes us towards
translating the participle here
in the passive voice
but even if one insists on translating it
in the middle voice it would not
change the interpretation
of the passage in light of the
overall truth of the entire
context of the passage

5) What if God wishes to make known the riches of His glory upon vessels of mercy, which He had appointed beforehand unto glory?

The point here, as well as the point of the entire passage, is that God is God, and that God is the sovereign potter and no one can tell Him what to do or question what He does. He will and can and does have mercy on whom He wills to have mercy, and He will and can and does harden whom He wills to harden. Salvation is not of man or by man, but of God who wills to show mercy and pardon as He pleases. This is undeniable in Scripture!

Conclusion   9:24-33

1. The effectual call to salvation has come to Jews and Gentiles 9:24

2. This inclusion of Jews and Gentiles in the true Israel of God was prophesied by Hosea and agreed upon by Isaiah   9:25-27

3. God will perform His will on earth 9:28

4. What can we say then?
    that the Gentiles
        the ones not seeking righteousness
            found righteousness by faith
    that the Jews
        the ones following the righteousness
            of the law missed true righteousness
                because they sought it by works
        they stumbled at Christ
            even as Isaiah promised
    but in the context of the passage
    it was all in accordance
        with the will of God

I realized, as we came to the end of our study, that we were overtime, but no one was in a hurry to leave right away. It was better to deal with the entire section in one setting. In fact, Dr. Sisk seemed to want us to stay around for a little longer, when he said, "Do you two men have a few more minutes that I could have with you?"

My heart responded quietly with the question, "Which problem does he want to discuss with us now?"

Chapter 20

Dr. Sisk didn't waste any time in telling us what the subject of our discussion was going to be, as he said, "I may have a problem in allowing you men to stay on the faculty here, even though I might want you to do so!"

I noted in my mind that he put it all in the realm of possibility. He might have a problem, and he might want us to stay, but even so, there was a problem. So I had to admit that it didn't sound good for us. I decided I would hit him with a direct question to get some direct answers.

"Are you saying you want us to stay now? Or is that question still up in the air? It might make a difference if you were in our corner, if something else is now getting in the way of our staying!" I noted.

"Well, both are possibilities. I have appreciated this study, and whether I agree or not, I have seen an attitude that is good, as we discuss these difficult matters. But I am still trying to make up my mind whether or not I want such strong views here on this campus by our teachers. Plus, I have several board members, as well as the dean of faculty, who would like to see you men dismissed as soon as possible, based on the theological issues," he admitted. "But on the other hand, there is the question of the damage it would do to the student body, if you left under duress!"

Dink and I both spoke, assuring him that we would have no part of any movement that would hurt the school, even if we were asked to leave, and that we had tried to squash any such upheaval that might be taking place now on campus, in light of the rumors which where floating around. He said he appreciated that attitude, and now almost wished he had never raised the issue, after he had gotten to know us. But the battle was almost blazing now, and he wasn't sure if he could douse the fire without greater repercussions than if we were to leave.

And then he added, "Not all men are as gracious as you men are! I wish I had known that before it became an issue! There may be nothing I can do to stop it now!"

Nothing was said about his son, for which I was glad! That too was up in the air and maybe out the window. No need for him to know how much his son was still upset with his parents, even so much that he didn't want to talk to anyone from the seminary faculty.

Dink and I left his office, still putting the whole situation in the Lord's hands, and even committed to the continuation of our morning vigil at the breakfast place. And it paid off after about a week of waiting, as Daryl did walk in again with his paper, and he came to Dink's booth, after buying his usual breakfast.

"Am I still welcome here?" he asked Dink meekly.

"Ya will be as long as I'm sittin' here!" Dink stated.

"Can I say I am sorry for the way I acted?" he wanted to know next.

"Sure can!" Dink said, while he still read his paper.

"Can we lay aside the papers and talk this morning?" he asked, as he unfolded his biscuit sandwich.

"If you'se is wantin' ta talk!" Dink assured him.

"Mr. Dink!" he said politely and humbly. "Why are some sons able to be close to their fathers and I am not?"

"Could be a lotta reasons! But I needs ta asks you a question! Was der ever a time when you was close or closer ta yer fadder dan you are now?" Dink probed.

"Yes, there was, but then something happened. And our relationship was never the same," he explained.

As they sat and talked, food was forgotten, as a young man was seeking to understand what had happened to his earlier relationship with his father. They were close when he was young, but when he reached his teen years, they drifted apart, and he didn't know why. He only knew that the time came when he couldn't stand to be around his dad. His father's attitude seemed different, but so was his. He couldn't remember if he was the one who changed or if his father was the one who had changed. All he knew was that their relationship got worse and worse, as the years went by. Finally, he had to leave home and break with both his parents and vow never to see them again, because his mother always backed his father!

He had concluded that he couldn't please his father anymore, no matter what he did, so why try. And this only made him more recalcitrant towards his father. He guessed the same was true of his father. As both of their attitudes became more hardened, neither one could stand to be around the other. He admitted that he felt sorry for his mother, as she tried to be a mediator of sorts at times, but she eventually backed his father in every situation.

And then he said, "Mr. Dink, I need help, but I don't know what to do, and I am not sure if I did know what needed to be done, whether or not I could do it!"

It was here that Dink went to the heart of the problem, as he asked him if he had ever really been saved, to which the boy answered no, he didn't think so! Dink spent the rest of the time explaining the gospel to him, telling him that the solution to his problem must begin with him dealing with his sin. Without that, they were shooting in the dark at dirty pigeons that would fly away for awhile, only to return to plague him again. Dink gave him one of the clearest presentations of the gospel I have ever heard!

When they parted, it was very obvious that God's grace was working in his life!

Chapter 21

After a few weeks off for the Christmas break, I began to realize that we would soon begin what might be my last semester at EBS. At this point of time, I was amazed at two things---how quickly the fall semester had flown by, and how serious the doctrinal issue at the seminary had become. I honestly wondered if Dink and I would survive as teachers through the spring semester, and to be honest, if we did survive that semester, it seemed now it would definitely be our last. I almost expected Dr. Sisk to cancel the rest of our study time together, in light of the human odds that seemed to be stacking up against us.

But my determination was clear, that as long as Dr. Sisk would allow us to meet, we would meet. In our next study, our first of the New Year, I wanted us to consider the subject of God's sovereignty and man's freedom. I sensed a need to review once again, since the last session was quite lengthy. I listed first the main thoughts we had been pursuing in our study.

1. God is sovereign over all things!

2. The will of man is not sovereign over any event, yet man acts freely and is a responsible being in all his actions!

   If someone besides God was sovereign over even a single event or action that takes place, then God would not be a sovereign God.

   Yes, men were responsible when they crucified Christ, even though they were carrying out the will of God, but

God was not the author of their sin, even though it came to pass in accordance with the will and purpose of God, as planned before the foundation of the world.

Even in Paul's discussion of Romans 9, he asserts both the sovereignty of God in salvation and the responsibility of man before God in man's rebellion against God, though men are clay vessels in the hands of a sovereign God.

Now we wanted to add another thought:

3. Though man is responsible, that does not mean he is able to do what God requires and commands him to do!

This is another of the problems we must face. How easy it is to jump to the conclusion that because man is responsible, he is able. But there are several lines of argumentation we can follow to show this is not true.

a. Are all men responsible to keep the Ten Commandments with perfection?

The answer to that has to be yes, for that is the basis whereby God will judge us. That is the basis whereby God sees us to be sinners. We all have broken the commandments of God. But what if a lost man told us he could not be considered by God to be a sinner, and he wasn't responsible before God to keep His commandments, because God knows and he knows that it is impossible for him to keep the commandments of God? And, since he is no longer responsible before God to keep His commands, because he is not able, God has no right to condemn him and consider his breaking of the commandments as sin. No ability means no responsibility according to this view!

No, clearly the Bible teaches that man is responsible, even though he is not able to keep God's commands. And is that not why Christ had to come and die for us, because we were responsible before God to keep His commandments, and we could not, and yet God at the same time held us accountable and responsible to do so?

b. Are all men responsible to repent and believe the Gospel?

The answer again is, yes, men are responsible to repent and to believe the gospel. But the question again is, are men able to repent and believe the gospel? The answer has to be no, in light of the sinfulness of man. Man not only lacks the ability to produce faith (faith is the gift of God), but he is also depraved in every area of his being, which causes him to center on himself and desire himself, and reject God, unless God enables him to do otherwise. Thus, a man is responsible to respond positively to the truth of the gospel by repentance and faith, but because he is a sinner, he is not able, just as he is not able to keep the Ten Commandments.

We have shown by illustration in two areas of man's spiritual accountability, that he is responsible, but responsibility does not necessarily include ability.

The question then becomes, if man is not able to produce faith in order to be saved, yet he is responsible, how can he be saved? The answer is that man is saved exactly the way Paul taught us in Romans 9---by the power and sovereignty of God alone based on His election of a people!

We have seen that responsibility does not equal ability, according to Scripture. We must understand that when the command of God comes to man to repent and believe the gospel, that God must give the ability, and He does in accordance with His sovereign will and power. Then, when man is saved, he can only say, "Look what God did! I give Him alone the glory!"

I thought at this point of a story in the Bible, which had helped me in my understanding of the subject. Jesus went into a synagogue, and he met there a man whose hand was paralyzed. The Pharisees, following Him, and always looking for a means of accusation against Him, asked if He thought it was lawful to heal on the Sabbath day. The text states clearly that they were asking Him this question for the explicit purpose that they might accuse Him. Jesus' reply was that surely a man, who had a sheep, which fell into a pit on the Sabbath, would lift it out of the pit. His rhetorical question and answer then became, "How much is a man better than a sheep? Therefore, it is lawful to do good on the Sabbath days." Then Jesus turned to the man, who had the paralyzed hand, and said to him, "Stretch forth your hand!" And he stretched forth his hand, and it was healed, and it was just like his other good hand.

Is there not a lesson here on man's inability and God's power for man to do that which he is unable to do in his own strength? Can we not properly suppose that this man would have stretched forth his hand to restore it to its normal state earlier in his life, if he could have? Thus, his inability is very clear. But here comes Christ to a helpless and powerless man, and tells him to do that which he is not capable of doing! The man could have replied to Christ, "Don't you know that I have been trying for many years to stretch forth this hand and couldn't! And now you come along and tell me to do that very thing---stretch it forth back to its original state? You must be kidding! That is an impossibility! Leave me alone! This hand will never be normal again!"

But the man did not say that, did he? He stretched forth his hand, and it was healed, and it did return to its normal state. But was it by the man's own power? No, it was only by the power of Christ, as the man believed the words of Christ, and responded, and both actions, the belief and the response, were by the power of Christ to fulfill the will of God. So it is in the matter of salvation. God calls us by an effectual call, and we respond by His power to fulfill His will for us as the elect of God. The sovereign potter is making a vessel for His glory in accordance with His will.

After several prolonged periods of discussion, we finally came to the end of our session. As we did, I couldn't help but wonder if Dr. Sisk would want to talk to us about his son once again, since it had been some time since we had met. I was glad when his secretary told him that there was a pressing phone call, which he needed to take. They had been calling him throughout our study, and she had promised he would be available immediately at the close of that hour.

Chapter 22

It was in the next few days that the matter of Dr. Sisk's son took another unexpected turn, as we found out more concerning the reason he had left home and why he had faked his own death. It all came out at one of the morning breakfasts.

Daryl suddenly looked up from his paper, as he and Dink were both eating and reading, and openly said, "Mr. Dink, I haven't been completely honest with you, as we have been talking about my problems!"

"Oh, is dat so?" Dink answered. "I kinda 'spected dat you was hidin' somethin' from me!"

"Yes, and I don't know quite how to tell you! It has to do with why I left home and why I faked my own death!"

"Faked yer own death, huh? I tink dat was kinda clear, too! But I guess der could be all kinds a reasons why! So rather dan we gets ourselves involved in some guessin' game, why dontcha just tell me!" Dink suggested.

"Well, to make it simple, I got a girl, to put it the best I can, in a family way almost two years ago. I met her when she was visiting over here on the East Coast at the beach, while I was there. She was a nice little girl too, and we just got carried away! When the week was over, I came home, and she went back to Minnesota, and of course, I had forgotten her, when the word came of her condition. I knew my parents would never understand it. So I picked a fight with them on purpose, and left home to go be with the girl, and even to marry her. I felt that was my duty!

"But after being there a few weeks, I knew it wasn't going to work. So I thought I could solve my problem by faking my death in a boat accident, which I did. I made sure that the boat blew up, but I had already gotten off of it, and then I swam to shore several miles away. No one knew up there that I was a long distance swimmer in high school, so they assumed I could never have made it to safety that far away from land. I then had a friend pick me up and take me a couple of hundred miles from there. Then, a bus took me even further. I changed my identity, so that no one could track me, as everyone thought I was dead.

"I figured that I had solved my problem, but still didn't want to see my parents, because there was too much explaining to do, which I didn't want to have to face. So I came here to live, seeing I didn't know anyone in Seminary City except my parents. I thought I could stay out of the places where they might go, get another new identity, change my looks, as much as I could, and start all over. Then maybe someday I could tell them the truth! But how, was my problem! And then you came along!"

"Was my commin' along good or bad?" Dink asked.

"Both, I guess! Bad, if I wanted to keep my false identity permanently! Good, if I wanted to just be me and face the music!" he reasoned. "I guess the best way to handle it would be to let the Lord take care of it!" he finally admitted.

"Yeah, but ya needs ta be saved before dat will ever come ta pass!" Dink warned.

"Mr. Dink! That's what I am weighing now! Do I want the Lord just so He will clean up my mess, or because He is Who He is? Would it be right for me to get saved, just so He could bail me out of trouble? I don't know if that would be the right thing to do or not? Maybe I had just better handle it myself!" he stupidly asserted.

"Ain't dat what's you been doin" all along, an' ain't dat what gotcha inta all dis mess ta begin wid?" Dink asked him.

Chapter 23

When he left us that morning, Daryl was still debating what he would do. We prayed that God would have His will in the boy's life. Someone might say at this stage, "What is the point of a Calvinist praying? Isn't it all going to work out in accordance with God's will anyway?" We pray because God has told us to pray. Prayer is our responsibility, and God has ordained that He will work through our prayers for the performance of His will. And a Calvinist always prays as Jesus did, "Thy will be done!

In reality it is the Arminian and the so-called modified Calvinist, who has no basis for prayer. God has done all He can to save men! Now He must wait for a man to respond! For God to do otherwise (to override the authority and power of a man's will), is to dehumanize a man, according to the Arminian. Such an action by God (again according to the Arminian) would be for God to coerce a man or to force a man, something which God would never do.

So the Calvinist asks the Arminian, why do you pray? God has already done everything He can to save a man, and now He must wait for a man to make up his own mind and exercise his own will before God can save him. For an Arminian to pray for God to send His power down in a service at church for the purpose of saving men is useless. All the power of God could be sent down on a service, but that power of God would never violate a man's will, according to the Arminian and his terms. The Calvinist would never use the word "violate" in relation to the salvation of a man. The Calvinist believes that the elect become willing in the day of God's power, therefore the

Calvinist can rightly pray for the power of God to fall upon a meeting of God's people and even lost people.

Someone has rightly said that all men are Calvinists, when they pray. They are asking God to do only that which God is capable of doing, when they pray for someone to be saved! In that matter it is a good thing that Arminians are not consistent, or they would never be able to pray for the lost. The very prayer they pray, and the fact that they pray, puts them in the Calvinist camp, whether they realize it or not. It is a pity, that when they get up off their knees, the Arminians go back, unknowingly, to their limiting of God and their elevating of man in their theological statements concerning salvation.

I took note at this point, that this needed to be a part of our discussion with Dink and Dr. Sisk, and it was at our next session, even in a more complete form than given above. Dr. Sisk seemed quite impacted by the above truth. Dink is always impacted by the truth! So we had a good session of study and the exchange of ideas.

After our time together, Dr. Sisk did update us on our status at the school, when he said, "The Chairman of our Executive Board is now insisting that you two men must go---immediately! And he seems to be building a considerable following among the board members. I don't know what to say. I feel so responsible for this! I wish they could all be in our study and see your attitudes concerning the matter. They think that the rumblings, which are being felt on campus about this issue, are being stirred by you men. I have tried to tell them, you are really seeking to quell the commotion, which is building. But they won't believe me. I don't know what is going to happen!" he said as he hung his head in sorrow.

"But dey ain't bigger dan God, is dey!" Dink declared.

Chapter 24

It was at our next breakfast (I say our, since I had joined Dink and Daryl by now at their booth), that Daryl professed faith in Christ. He had made a profession, when he was a child in one of those super, high-powered children's services with much hype and high-pressure. But from all we could tell, he had never been saved, and we were very careful that he now had truly come to know Christ, which as far as we could tell, he had. But then came the difficult part, as Dink immediately faced him with his present responsibility.

"Ya knows whatcha needs ta do now, dontcha?" Dink queried.

"Yes, I need to go home to my parents and tell them all about the reason I left, and that it really had nothing to do with them or anybody else. It was entirely my fault! They will be shocked, and who knows what else they might say or think. But I have to do all I can to make right what has been wrong for so many months in my relationship with them," he admitted.

"Den, whatcha gotta do?" Dink asked.

"I will need to go to Minnesota and turn myself in to the police there, admitting my deception, and I also need to go to the girl and her family to make things right with them, whatever it takes."

"Anyting else?" Dink asked.

"Just to keep my heart open to the Lord, as He leads me through this thing, and be willing to take responsibility for my sin, as I try to set everything straight with Him and others. I know He has saved me, but there is so much I need to deal with now to have His fullness of blessing!" he said with a hopeful smile on his face.

"When does ya wants ta see yer folks?" Dink asked.

"As soon as possible! The sooner I do what I should, the sooner God will begin to unravel this whole thing!" he declared confidently again. Then he added, "Can you men go with me and help me do this? It's not that I fear my parents, but that I don't know exactly how they will react. Should we all just show up at their door, or should we let them know we are coming, or what?" he wondered.

"I tink it might be best ifs da Preacha an' I tell yer dad dat you's been found an' ya wants ta come home. Den he can prepare yer mom. Dat way dey can be prepared fer da meetin' whens we come!" Dink suggested.

"Well, then why don't we do this," he said with careful thought. "I probably need a few days to get myself ready, so why don't you tell my dad after the next study that you have with him, that I am coming home, and then we can go see them that evening. That will give them time to prepare their emotions as well. I would hate to walk in cold on them with no allowance for the preparation of their hearts and minds for that moment."

We all agreed on this arrangement, and so the clock began to point to the day after tomorrow with one side of the fracture knowing it and the other side longing to learn something, but unaware that the hoped-for day would be sooner than they could imagine.

"Can I ask one more thing of you, Dr. Pointer and Dr. Dink? Will you go with me to Minnesota and help me talk to the authorities there, as well as to the girl and her family? It is going to be scary enough to see everyone again, she and her family, and the police! But it might be even more frightful to face a judge, if that is necessary. I don't even have a lawyer or someone to plead for me!"

"You do now!" I said, looking at Dink.

Chapter 25

It was two days later that we met once again with Dr. Sisk for our study. But unknown to him, it was also to share with him the news of his son. I wondered if I could concentrate on the study properly, in light of the anticipation of the second event.

I had decided once again to summarize for us the simple outline that we were following in the unfolding of our subject. I listed the main points and a few sub points as follows:

1. God is sovereign over all things!

2. The will of man is not sovereign over any event, yet man acts freely and is a responsible being in all his actions!

3. Though man is responsible, that does not mean he is able to do what God requires and commands him to do!

   a. All men are responsible to keep the Ten Commandments, although they are not able.

   b. All men are responsible to repent and believe the gospel, although they are not able.

4. The Calvinistic system is the most encouraging and powerful basis for prayer and missions and evangelism, even more so than the Arminian system of theology!

   a. Prayer
   b. Missions and Evangelism

We had dealt with 4a in the previous hour of study, so we now turned to 4b, an area where so many had challenged Calvinism.   I began by making several foundational statements.

1. No church or Christian should authorize any kind of an evangelistic approach or missions program on the basis of pragmatism---that is the idea that the best program and approach is the one that gets the most decisions or results, or builds the biggest church!

    This should be obvious to any sincere Christian. It is easy to get decisions by means of high pressure, and humanistic methods, and even by trimming the gospel message. But that is not what God wants us to do---to fill his church with lost people. In fact, Jesus in John 6 had gathered a large following in the beginning of His ministry, but He completely shut it down, because He knew many were following him just for the loaves and the fishes, that is for the physical benefits.

    For that reason, Jesus thinned his crowd, so it only contained His immediate disciples, when He told the crowd following Him that to be His disciples they must eat His flesh and drink his blood. These were words, which had figurative meaning, that is, that His disciples would be those in a spiritual relationship with Him, and they would receive their life from Him, and continue to draw upon Him for their spiritual life and strength.

    This surely must have puzzled His close disciples, and perhaps they even wondered what He was doing---running off His crowd. For many of the mega-church builders of our day, it would have been a major marketing failure. No wonder His disciples of those early days of ministry were so puzzled over this situation, that Jesus asked them if they were going away also. But they admitted that they had nowhere else to go. Which is to say that they were not certain what He was doing, but they knew that He had the words of life. But His methodology---they didn't understand that! And this is no doubt the reason that His church has struggled for years over methods of ministry---some just cannot see what is wrong with a method if it gets results. Even the trimming of the gospel message in certain areas is acceptable to many today, if that will help get results!

But numbers cannot be our standard of ministry methodology. The producing of true disciples must be the gauge and goal of every method we use. And this is what Arminianism is often accused of---using pragmatic methods when it comes to ministry methodology. This certainly is not to paint every Arminian with the same brush, but can we not see that Arminian theology encourages some to practice false methods of evangelism?

If we be believe that salvation is in the hands of man, that is, that God has done all He can do to save a man; and God must wait upon man to start the ball of salvation rolling before He can step in and do His part; does that thinking not even unconsciously lead toward the use of any and every means and method, which might possibly encourage a man to exercise his mind and will towards "deciding" for Jesus? Scare him enough, shame him enough, pressure him enough, emotionalize him enough, scold him enough, promise him enough, etc. and etc.---anything to get his will to make a decision now.

This is not to say that true evangelism doesn't touch a man's emotions, or show him his sin, or challenge him to be saved. But the above speaks of the possibility of an over-zealousness that does not depend on the Holy Spirit and the Word of God, but depends on the persuasive power and methods of men to cause a man to respond, when there is no real work of the Spirit of God present. All of this because we feel we must and can do something in the strength of man (though we sometimes think such is by the power of God) to cause a man to make a decision for Christ by his own strength. Is this not acceptable, if done on the Arminian presupposition that God has done all he can do, till man in his strength exercises faith? Are we not helping God by helping this man make a decision?

Just take a look at the churches of today. Many church members are so shallow in their understanding of the truth, that they couldn't even tell you the plan of salvation. Yet they claim they are right with God! Others can tell you the plan of salvation, but their lives betray their doctrinal knowledge, as they give little evidence of true salvation. Many others are members and have been members and continue to be members of churches, as they were swept into a church during a time of pressure and emotionalism, and were even baptized, but after a few weeks or months of attendance, they drifted back into the old life. Some even have a name for these evangelistic failures---carnal Christians---someone who lives like a lost man, but is still a Christian, so they say, because he did at one time make a profession of faith in Christ.

So much of this has come, because we have thought that we must do something in our power to nudge men to make a decision in their own power. Remember again, that God has done all He can do, according to the Arminian view, to save a man, and He must wait for man to cooperate with Him to be saved. We are told by Arminians that God will never force a man's will! Therefore, God is powerless until man responds. Yet it seems all right, according to some, for us to help force or coerce a man's will in some way to choose salvation.

2. The Calvinist has a far different motivation and basis for engaging in the work of evangelism and missions!

God has a people out there in this world---yea, in every part of the world. It is the responsibility of the church and of Christians to go into all the world and preach the gospel, challenging men to believe the gospel. But the Calvinist does not depend on his methodology to get decisions for Christ. He depends upon the power of God to call out His elect, as the gospel is preached. Clearly, the human pressure of results and getting decisions is not on the Calvinist preacher and witness, for he is simply the agent in declaring the truth, which in turn has the power to save.

Again, the Calvinist does not go hoping he can get some decisions by his own ability to preach or persuade, but he knows that God will do the work. God will call out the elect. God will convict men. God will challenge men. God will effectually call His elect to Himself. God will enlighten their hearts and minds. God will teach men the reality of the truth. God will persuade men of sin and the way of salvation. God will save His elect as we go and preach and teach the truth.

Is this not a more solid basis and ground for missions and evangelism than the Arminian foundation--- dependence upon God and His power rather than thinking we must depend upon ourselves or even the men to whom we preach for the results? Will this not give the missionary more desire to go, more encouragement to stay, more boldness to speak, more confidence to endure hardship, etc., than the Arminian thought that we must by our own arguments and abilities persuade men of their need of Christ?

Our time was passing us by like a silver zephyr on an unrestricted train track, and so I had to bring our study to a halt. But how would I get from this to the discussion of Dr. Sisk's son, especially when his secretary let him know there was a pressing phone call awaiting him again. We did excuse ourselves from his office, so he would have some privacy for the call, but we waited outside, as we had requested a few more minutes of his time. But our wait turned out to be a half an hour. And all Dink and I could do was sit and twiddle our thumbs as we waited rather impatiently, because of the unique circumstances.

Finally, we were invited back into his office, and I began with the words, "The Lord has found your son!"

Chapter 26

Dr. Sisk's face remained very stoic, as he received the news of his son. But this did not mean that he had no questions. After establishing that his son Daryl was in Seminary City, and that he wanted to see his parents, and that he had been saved, Dink and I felt we had told Dr. Sisk all that was necessary for us to discuss with him at this time. We sensed the need to leave the rest of the story of his days away from home with Daryl. He could tell them both in his own way, and it would no doubt mean more to them, if it came from him, as they could see the attitude of his heart in the process. It was agreed that we would bring him by their home about 7:00 that evening. Dr. Sisk said he would share the information with his wife.

When 7:00 came that evening, Dink, and I, and Daryl were standing at the front door of the Sisk home. We didn't even have to knock, however, because the door was already open, and both parents were standing there with open arms and tearful eyes, as mother, father and son all stood for awhile just hugging each other, as if they never wanted to turn loose of one another again. Following that moving moment, Daryl told them the full story of his reason for leaving home, assuring them that the fault was entirely his and none of theirs. Then came the story of the young lady, and the faked death in a boat explosion and of his return to Seminary City and even of our working with him at the breakfast hour. He told the story with the fullest of details, even laughing when he unfolded our plan to secretly befriend him, in order to minister to him.

It was really one of the most precious evenings I have ever spent! I even thought I saw traces of the man I had known years ago, when Dr. Sisk had ministered to me as a young college student, as his attitude changed dramatically as Daryl spoke. Though it was a very sober moment, it was also a joyful time, and that is what stirred my memory of those days, when I had known him previously. Plus, the Sisks could not thank us enough, that is, Dink and me, for the help we had given to their son in his restoration to them and the salvation of their son in his spiritual life.

When we told them we would accompany him back to Minnesota, so he could set the records straight, they understood and agreed that it was the right thing to do. They only hoped that the matter could be settled easily, but whatever the situation, it was right for him to take responsibility for what he had done, and to do whatever the authorities demanded, and whatever was right regarding the young lady. When they asked about the need of a lawyer, we told them that Mac Turnover of Turnover News Agency had offered one of his lawyers to help him at no or at least minimal charges.

As we left that evening, there was the agreement and understanding, that Daryl would not be moving home, since his future was a little uncertain, as far as what the authorities would require of him. And besides, he was already committed to a lease on the apartment, where he was now staying. But there was the assurance that he would be going to church with them every Sunday, and spending much time with them at their home, when the legal matters were settled.

As Dink and I finally were leaving the celebration, Dr. Sisk pulled us aside to reiterate his thanks. I wouldn't have mentioned our situation at the school, but he did, as he said, "I want you men to know that if you are forced to leave the school, I will stand with you!"

I couldn't help but wonder what he meant by that?

Chapter 27

It took Daryl a few days to make the arrangements to return to Minnesota, in order that he might deal with the mess that he had made and left there. He had decided not to make any calls ahead of him, but thought it would be better if he showed up and made his confession, and then let them deal with it. He wasn't sure they would let him come in on his own, if he let them know ahead of time. And the same was true of the young lady and her family.

This gave us the opportunity to meet for another of our study sessions, which were going to be continued, even though Dr. Sisk had opened up to us and wanted us to stay at the school. He said he wanted to learn as much as he could about what we believed, just in case he had to go to bat for us before the board or anyone else, in light of the situation he himself had created for us.

I had decided that we would next deal with the sovereignty of God in calling out His chosen ones, the elect, centering on the effectual call of irresistible grace. This is surely seen as an impossible doctrine by so many, just as the other points of our study in the area of Calvinism. But the question is again, does the Scripture teach the doctrine of an effectual call to the elect by God's irresistible grace?

I called our attention again to the fact that so many times men take one verse in the Bible and use it as their interpretive principle, as they would seek to understand many other passages of the Bible from that one verse. One such passage is John 3:16. Yet, often such people totally ignore the teaching of many other verses in the Bible, and in the case of John 3:16, they ignore even some key verses of the gospel of John itself!

Which means if and when you give someone a difficult verse concerning God's sovereignty in salvation, they shout out, "What about John 3:16? Don't forget John 3:16?" This means that any and every verse in the Bible has to be governed by their understanding and explanation of that one verse. Sometimes a Calvinist wants to say, "What about John 10? Don't forget John 10!" Or "What about Ephesians 1? Don't forget about Ephesians 1!" Men's minds are so set, it seems, to defend the will and power of man, that they totally ignore other passages in the Bible, which clearly teach the sovereignty of God in all things, including salvation.

What About John 10?

I told our group that I would like to raise that question! What about John 10 and its teaching of the Shepherd's irresistible call to His sheep? Do not verses 1-6 teach that only the sheep hear the voice of the shepherd, when He comes to call them out of the fold? They hear and know His voice, and the other sheep do not, and He brings them out when He calls them, because they know His voice and they will not follow the voice of a stranger.

Does not Jesus teach in this passage the following?

1. That there are many false shepherds!

2. That there is one true shepherd (the Lord Jesus Himself)!

3. That the doorkeeper of the sheepfold opens the door of the sheepfold to the true shepherd!

4. That the true shepherd comes into the sheepfold and calls out His sheep!

5. That the true sheep and only the true sheep (God's elect) hear the voice or call of the true shepherd!

6. That the true sheep will not (emphatic negative in the Greek language) follow the voice or call of a stranger!

7. That the true sheep will flee from the voice of a stranger, because they know it is not the voice of the true shepherd!

8. That this is speaking of the effectual call of God to His elect for their salvation!

9. That those who heard this parable of Christ did not understand what He was saying, and, thus, should it be any surprise to us when men do not understand these doctrines today?

Plus, there are other verses, which clearly teach this effectual and irresistible call. One of the clearest is I Corinthians 1:18-31, where Paul lays down the following truths:

1. The preaching of the cross is to them that are perishing foolishness! 18

2. The preaching of the cross is the power of God to us who are saved! 18

3. The wisdom of man is powerless in this work of salvation!   19

4. The wisdom of man is foolishness to God!   20

5. The world by its wisdom does not know God!   20

6. It pleases God by the foolishness of preaching (foolish to men) to save them that believe!   21

7. Men are impressed more by other means than by the preaching of the cross---the Jews require a sign and the Greeks seek after wisdom!   22

8. But Paul preaches Christ crucified, which he admits is to the Jews a stumbling block and to the Greeks foolishness!   23

9. But unto them who are called, both Jews and Greeks, Christ is the power of God and the wisdom of God---it is the effectual call of God that makes the difference!   23

10. For you see your calling, brethren, how that not many wise men after the flesh (are called), not many mighty men (are called), not many noble men (are called)! 26

11. But God has chosen the foolish things of the world to confound the wise men, and God has chosen the weak things of the world to confound the mighty, and God has chosen the base things of the world, and things that are despised, yea, even things which

are not, to bring to NOTHING the things that are!
27-28

12. And why has God chosen such people? So that no
flesh should glory in His presence. So that we all
would acknowledge that Christ Jesus is made unto
us wisdom and righteousness and sanctification and
redemption! 29-30

13. So that if we glory, we will glory in the Lord! 31

Can it be denied that these verses speak of an effectual
call to salvation? God has chosen certain people (verses
12-31), and these are the ones who come to Him. These are
the ones who believe in Him. The call does not come by
the wisdom or power of man, but by the power of the
gospel, which men see as foolishness. We might be able to
impress men by other means (signs and wisdom), but this is
not that which is the power of God unto salvation. The
power of God unto salvation comes by the preaching of
Christ crucified, and in that process God calls out those
whom He has chosen. And this is what gives God the
glory, as it recognizes God as the power of salvation from
the beginning to the end---salvation is of the Lord!

When we had finished, Dr. Sisk thanked us again for
what we had done for his son. Then he gave us further bad
news! The Dean of the Faculty, Dr. Welsh, was working
behind the scenes with those board members who were
desirous to get rid of us. It was a very sneaky thing for him
to do, but Dr. Sisk didn't want to confront him---yet! But
he promised he would in time! And so the plot thickens!

Chapter 28

It was several days later that Daryl and Dink and I left for Minnesota---cold Minnesota in the wintertime! We didn't know quite what to expect when we got there, but we bathed the trip in prayer, and took off for places known but events unknown. We were met at the airport by Mac and his lawyer, as they had just flown in also. When I asked him what he was doing there (I really hadn't expected him), he replied that he had come to help a friend of a friend, and then he smiled, when he said, "And there might even be a story in this for us!"

We got our luggage and then got into the rental car, which Mac had waiting for us, and we headed out through the snow into the northern regions of Minnesota, the land of a thousand lakes. We had decided we would go to the police station first, lest someone would recognize Daryl, if we went elsewhere, and then there was no telling what might happen. I could envision police cars stopping us all, and taking us all to jail for harboring a man they thought was dead, but who was really a fugitive.

The area where it had all taken place was a typical Northern community, with a small police station, which no doubt was rather surprised, when five of us walked into the station that morning and broke some shocking news to them. Daryl took the lead, as he stated matter of factly, "I am Daryl Sisk, and I have come to turn myself in!"

The poor lady behind the window at the reception area said with some surprise, "You are who? And you are turning yourself in for what?"

"I am Samuel Simmons, though that is not my real name. My real name is Daryl Sisk, and I am the young man who some months ago was supposedly killed in an explosion in my boat out on Little Big Lake! I am turning myself in with the explanation that I faked my death, and I am really still alive!" Daryl tried again.

"Have you got some identification?" she then asked, trying to get her wits about her and be more professional about the whole situation.

Daryl pulled out some documents, and after he handed them to her, she spent a few moments pouring over them. Then she turned to us and asked, "And who are all of you people?"

The poor lady must have gotten another shock, when Dink spoke up in his unique vernacular and stated, "Da two of us is his friends," he said, as he pointed to me and to himself. "Den dat guy over der is his lawyer, an' dat other one der is anudder friend, Mac Turnover, of Turnover News Agency!"

Not only was Dink a shock to her, but the mention of a lawyer and someone as big as Turnover News Agency, must have made her wonder what she had gotten herself into that morning. For someone who had probably expected a routine day, this suddenly may have become the biggest day in the life of that small police station. It didn't take her long after that to call for help, and soon several other policemen were standing around us, asking questions.

Finally, they decided they had better lock Daryl up until they could get some counsel from the chief of police, who hadn't gotten in yet and maybe even some counsel from their District Attorney's office. After all, it's not every day that a supposed dead man, who has faked his death in an explosion on his own boat, walks into the room and wants to undo all that he has done illegally and gotten away with. Has he broken any laws? What laws has he broken? As far as they were concerned, the books were closed on Samuel

Simmons death, and maybe some of them even wished it had stayed that way!

While they shuffled Daryl off to a cell, until they could determine what they should do with him, we got the directions to the young lady's house, and Dink and I set off to find her and her parents. We decided that just two of us would go there, lest the parents and the girl be scared out of their wits and get the wrong impression by the presence of a lawyer and a news mogul appearing suddenly in their living room! When we rang the doorbell, a young lady answered it, which we assumed was Daryl's friend! Since it seemed that no one else was at home, and since we had no idea how she would receive us, we stood at the door and tried to introduce ourselves with Dink doing the talking.

"Mam, I understands dat ya knew a young man named Samuel Simmons!" he began, getting right to the point of the subject.

She nodded with a puzzled look on her face, but said nothing, probably because she didn't know how to answer such a question.

"Well, Mam!" Dink started again, as if he were searching for the next words, something I had never seen him do very often before. "We came ta tell ya dat he is still alive, and wants ta make tings right wid ya."

Now she was shocked! And she was the one looking for words, as well! But, finally, they came pouring out like water from a broken levy, when she said, "Still alive? How can that be? He was killed in a boat explosion! How do you know he is still alive, and where is he now?" she asked.

"He's in da local jail now here in yer town. Don't know what dey will do wid him! But he'd like ta see ya, as soon as he can! He's become a Christian, an' now he wants ta do what's right concernin' everyting! Dat's why he came an' turned hisself inta da police---ta make everyting right wid God an' you all!" Dink said.

About then her mother came to the door, and we were invited into the house. Dink went over it all again with her mother, who also was as equally shocked. They seemed to be a rather solid middle class people. The house was very tidy and well kept. The mother seemed to have some solid characteristics about her---easy to talk to, the ability to understand what was going on, a real concern for her daughter, openness to hear what we were saying, and some real interest in the news about Daryl. I saw no bitterness in her or the daughter, when we mentioned his name.

The daughter was a pretty little girl with a sweet spirit, so it seemed. And there did seem also to be a real joy that Daryl was still alive! We didn't see the baby, so we said nothing about that subject for now. And then the girl asked an interesting question, when she said, "Do you think I could see Daryl at the police station?"

Her mother jumped in at that point, and nixed the question by saying, "Don't you think it's a little too early for anything like that? After all, you barely know the boy!"

I thought I sensed some bitterness at this point from the mother's perspective, but then, one could surely understand such, if that was the case. I decided that I probably would have felt the same way, were I in her place. So when the daughter said nothing in answer to her mother's statement, we followed suit.

But I was determined to do one thing before we left the home---ask about the baby, which I did. And I wasn't surprised when I received an answer.

"The baby was put up for adoption! We thought that was the best thing for all involved!" the mother answered.

Chapter 29

Since the authorities had not decided what to do with Daryl, nor would they decide for a few days, Dink and I decided to go back to Seminary City. This would enable us to teach our classes and also to meet with Dr. Sisk on our normal schedule. So, after visiting with Daryl in jail for an hour or so on Sunday, we left in the early afternoon to return home. Mac told us if we needed to travel back the next weekend, we could so at his expense. He would leave the lawyer in Minnesota, just in case Daryl might need him.

When back in Seminary City on Monday afternoon, we made our weekly visit to the president's office for our study. But even before that, we shared with him the whole situation about his son. He said if we went up the next weekend, he would try to go with us. After prayer, we were into our study of further truths from John 10:11, which speak of Christ's death for His sheep.

John 10:11

I am the good shepherd: the good shepherd giveth his life for the sheep.

John 10:14-15

14 I am the good shepherd, and know my sheep, and am known of mine. 15 As the Father knoweth me, even so know I the Father: and I lay down my life for the sheep.

John 10:17-18

17 Therefore doth my Father love me, because I lay down my life, that I might take it again. 18 No man taketh it from me, but I lay it down of myself. I have power to lay it down, and I have power to take it again. This commandment have I received of my Father.

If there is one thing these verses teach, it is that Christ did not come to this earth in a willy-nilly manner to die with the hope that someone would accept His sacrifice for their sin, but yet maybe no one would, which was the other possibility. Clearly He died for His sheep! Note clearly what these verses say.

1. Christ is the Good Shepherd!

2. The Good Shepherd knows His sheep from the others!

3. The Good Shepherd's sheep know Christ!

4. The Good Shepherd gives/lays down His life for the sheep!

5. The Good Shepherd lays down His life that He may take it up again!

6 No man takes the Good Shepherd's life from Him, but He lays it down of Himself.

7. The Good Shepherd has power to lay down His life and He has power to take it up again.

Do not these points taken from the noted verses in John 10 make it very clear that Christ was in control of His death in every aspect, including the purpose for which He died--- for His sheep? He died for His sheep (His elect or chosen ones as noted in our last chapter). He rose for His sheep!

He knows His sheep and they know Him. He does all of this of His own accord and for a purpose---the purpose for which His Father sent Him to this earth---to save a people.

Paul states this truth in another way in Ephesians 5:25 that Christ loved the church and gave himself for it! Who is the church? The ecclesia---the called out ones, and Paul has made it clear in Ephesians 1 that they were chosen on the basis of God's will and not on the basis of anything good in them, nor on the basis of their choice.

Now, again, I can hear someone cry out, what about such and such a verse or verses in the Bible! But I would say in return, what about John 10? And what about Ephesians 5:25? Do these verses not say that Christ died in some unique manner for His sheep---for His church---for His chosen and called out ones? Explain that to me! I am simply saying that the death of Christ had a unique meaning and power and application and purpose for the sheep, which it does not have to the non-elect. This truth certainly goes with what we have already seen in John 10, and when one puts it all together, there is no denying the reality of the death of Christ having a special meaning and reference for His sheep.

I handed Dr. Sisk some further notes that I had on the subject, ones I had made when he had guided me in my study on Calvinism at Baptist College years ago. I suggested that he might want to review these in more depth with reference to the interpretation of particular verses, which many use to claim that Christ died for all men in the same manner. (The reader at this point may want to see *A Journey in Grace* on this subject, Richbarry Press, 1990).

After further explanation, our discussion turned to the matter of Daryl and further understanding of the weekend we had spent with him in Minnesota.

Chapter 30

After we had finished with a thorough report to Dr. Sisk on the situation with Daryl, Dr. Sisk seemed pressed to say something to us about our situation at the school.

"We have two major situations on campus, which really trouble me concerning you two men!" he stated frankly. "First, the board is getting stronger in their opposition against you, thanks to Dr. Welsh, and secondly, the student concern is growing as well, in anticipation of what they are hearing about the matter, though this issue was never intended to be made known to them. I wish I had never opened this can of worms! I am so sorry and I do apologize to you for this whole sad mess! I know it has put you both in a very unfair position. Do you have any suggestions, as to what I can do to quell this potential uproar on campus and among the board members? Strange, isn't it, that the students are on one side of this issue, and a great number of the board members are on the other side?"

We assured him not to worry about it, that the Lord would lead us concerning the future, whenever He wanted it to be brought to a head. In the meantime we would seek to calm the student concern, and he would be the one to do likewise concerning the troubled board members. Just share with them what he had learned about us and our beliefs and our attitude in our discussions of the subject of our concern. We reminded him that he was still president of the school, and perhaps he should consider very strongly the need of a meeting with Dr. Welsh!

We then asked him if there was anyone on the board, who would be in our corner---someone who knew us well and our doctrinal views. To my surprise he said a new man's name had been added, a Jasper Showers, from

Georgia, and he seemed to know us well, though many knew us from afar. Dink and I both were shocked, elated and encouraged by this bit of knowledge. Surely, there was only one Jasper Showers---our good friend of some years ago, who we had helped through a rough time in his life. Also, he was the father of April Showers, my son's girlfriend, and the reason my gasoline bill was so high some months. (See *A Journey in Salvation*)

As Dink and I walked back across campus, we noticed some posters up in very conspicuous places, announcing a meeting for the noon hour that day. I must say, we did not appreciate them, because it told of a noon meeting in a certain area of the school cafeteria to discuss what was termed "Hyper-Calvinism!" But then it also said, "Anyone Welcome!" I looked at Dink and he looked at me, and neither one of us had to say one word about where we would be during the noon hour that day.

When I got back to my office, I called Dr. Sisk and asked him if he knew anything about such a meeting, and following a moment of shock and speechlessness, he too stated clearly where he would be during that noon hour as well. When I got off the phone, I walked back to the place where one of the announcements was posted, to see if it had anything on it concerning who was sponsoring the meeting. But there was no student group or faculty names attached to the sign---only the announcement of the gathering, along with the subject and place of meeting.

On that basis one could only guess who might be sponsoring such a meeting. Was it some Calvinists? Was it the Arminians? Was it the ones who called themselves Moderate Calvinists? Or perhaps the whole thing was a joke, as someone was making fun of the whole situation, which was jarring the campus? We would soon know!

Chapter 31

I must say, Dink and I were very surprised, when we found our way into the room where the noon meeting was supposed to take place---no one was there! Perhaps, we were early, which was a trait of both of us, and students, we noted, were usually late to such meetings. But then when the announced hour did arrive, just one student came into the room, and it was someone neither Dink nor I knew.

We all looked at each other, all three of us, and the questions began to fly? Is this the right meeting place? Has the meeting been canceled? If so, who cancelled it, and better yet, who called the meeting to begin with? Dink and I introduced ourselves to the only other attendee, and he was very friendly and seemed glad to meet us. After a brief time of fellowship, we decided there was to be no meeting, so we parted very cordially, passing through the rest of the cafeteria as we left the dining area.

But when I got back to my office, I had an idea, but as I thought further, I decided I had better check with Dr. Sisk to see if he would give me permission to do such a thing. Why not have a meeting on hyper-calvinism? Someone had either played a joke on us, or had canceled such a meeting at the last minute, for who knows what reason. So why not put up other signs all over campus, and have a discussion tomorrow in one of the rooms adjoining the dining area on the subject of hyper-calvinism?

Dr. Sisk agreed to the idea, and he didn't even mention any set restrictions. Dink was ecstatic when I talked to him about it, and he said he would take care of the preparation and distribution of the advertising of the meeting. I told him clearly to put our names as the ones who would be leading the meeting, or people would think the signs were put out by whoever pulled the stunt the previous day. So, it was all set---tomorrow at noon there WOULD BE a meeting to discuss hyper-calvinism.

The next morning when I got into my office to prepare for my classes, there were several phone calls from various faculty members and one from the Dean of Faculty. He wanted to know who had authorized me to have such a meeting, and when I told him that Dr. Sisk had done so, he didn't seem to be a happy camper, and insisted I tell him what we were doing. So I told him we were going discuss hyper-calvinism, and if he wanted to know more, to come and meet with us, and he would be welcome.

Even a few students called or stopped by the office, and all who did so were positive about the meeting, and even excited about it. One said we might even have to move to the chapel, the announcement was creating such a stir. When I had to walk across the campus to my first class, I came to understand why there was such a stir over the meeting. Dink and whoever worked with him (he could not have done it all by himself), had posters plastered everywhere, large and small, even with catchy phrases inviting people to come and learn about hyper-calvinism.

But the one call that I enjoyed the most was from the faculty member who had been the most critical of us, even in his classes, to the point of falsely representing our view, calling me a hyper-calvinist. He too wanted to know what we were doing. He thought this might be in response to the little joke he and some of the students had played on us yesterday, he actually admitted, when they announced a meeting to discuss hyper-calvinism, just to see if we would show up. I answered by telling him, yes, that's where we got the idea, and for all he knew, our announcement was a joke also.

Chapter 32

As the noon hour approached, Dink's statement about having to move to another room came true, except for one problem---there was no other room. There had been such a stir on campus, because of the false advertising of a meeting, that the reality of a true such meeting packed our room till it was over-flowing. I passed out a copy of the following to each person present. This was the first chart I would present to discuss the subject of Calvinism and Arminianism.

The Understanding of Some Concerning the Subject!

Column 1 ARMINIANISM	Column 2 <MODIFIED>	Column 3 CALVINISM	Column 4 EXTREME CALVINISM
Five Point Arminianism			Extreme Calvinism
		WHAT	
Depravity Not Total	<Arminian		Total Depravity
		IS	
Conditional Election	<Arminian		Uncondi- tional Election
		A	
General Atonement	<Arminian		Particular Atonement
		TRUE	
Resistible Grace	<Arminian		Irresistible Grace
		CALVINIST?	
No Persever- ance of Saints	<Arminian Calvinistic>		Perseverance of the Saints

EXPLANATION OF THE CHART

COLUMN 1
This column represents true five point Arminianism!

COLUMN 2
This column represents what some are trying to call modified Calvinism. But it is really a modified Arminianism, because this view is either a five point Arminianism or for some a four point Arminianism (some believe in eternal security and are weak on perseverance, which might make them four and a half point Arminians). There is no way such a view can call itself Calvinism in any sense, and to do so is absolutely false!

COLUMN 4
This is really true Calvinism, but some again are falsely labeling true Calvinism as extreme or hyper-calvinism, which is not only incorrect but dishonest and misleading!

COLUMNS 3-4
This shows the fallacy of what happens when one calls himself a modified Calvinist, and then also falsely seeks to make true Calvinism into a hyper or extreme Calvinism! When he is finished he has no definition of a true Calvinist!

I gave a little further explanation as follows. The only point where it seems the view as pictured above as modified Calvinism might qualify as a Calvinist would be on the fifth point, which means he would be an Arminian on four out of the five points. And then it would all depend also on how he explained that fifth point, whether he would be Arminian or Calvinistic in some sense on that point. But it is clear that there is no way such a person could ever be called even a modified or a moderate Calvinist. He would either be an Arminian or a modified Arminian!

A Proper Understanding of the Subject!

ARMINIANISM	<MODIFIED> ARMINIAN-ISM	TRUE CALVINISM	EXTREME CALVINISM
Five Point Arminianism	(Called Falsely Modified Calv.)	Five Point Calvinism	Extreme Calvinism
Depravity Not Total	<Arminian	Total Depravity	Total Depravity
Conditional Election	<Arminian	Uncondi-tional Election	Uncondi tional Election
General Atonement	<Arminian	Particular Atonement	Particular Atonement
Resistible Grace	<Arminian	Irresistible Grace	Irresistible Grace
No Persever-ance of Saints	<Arminian Calvinistic>	Perseverance of the Saints	Perseverance of the Saints
Human Responsibility	Human Responsibiity	Human Responsibility	Denial of Human Res-ponsibility
Missions and Evangelism a Necessity	Missions and Evangelism a Necessity	Missions and Evangelism a Necessity	Missions and Evangelism Unnecessary
Free Offer of the Gospel	Free Offer of the Gospel	Free Offer of the Gospel	No Free Offer of the Gospel

EXPLANATION OF THE CHART

One should be able to understand the chart through the five
points, which is the same format as the first chart, but a correct
statement of these points of thought. It is the extra three points,
which need, perhaps, a little explanation.

That which distinguishes hyper-Calvinism or extreme-Calvinism
from all the other views are the last three areas on the chart.

Arminianism, modified Arminianism and Calvinism
all believe in human responsibility
(the responsibility of all men to believe the gospel
and of the church to take the gospel out to every creature),
and missions and evangelism as a necessity,
and in the free offer of the gospel to every person.

It is the fourth column
of extreme-Calvinism or hyper-Calvinism
which denies the last three areas of truth---
(1) human responsibility
(2) evangelism and missions,
(3) the true offer of the gospel to every person

True Calvinism does not deny these truths,
and that is what distinguishes and separates
a true Calvinist
from a hyper-calvinist or an extreme-calvinist!!!

As I set forth the explanation of these charts, I sought to
do so objectively. We were there to understand the view,
not argue over it. I then opened the floor for questions with
some restrictions. We would discuss this subject
objectively not subjectively or argumentatively. Even if
someone disagreed with my presentation, the question must
be set forth objectively, or it would not be accepted!

Much to my surprise, most everyone abided by my suggested restrictions, and we had a good discussion of the whole matter. No one's blood boiled! No one got upset! No one made any false accusations! No one wanted to shout me down! No one called me names! No one asked any questions, which were out of bounds! And no one asked any questions about the rumors concerning me and Dink and our future at the school. Even Dr. Welsh seemed to sober up some in the process.

When the session was over, a number of people thanked me for clarifying some issues for them, even though they weren't sure they agreed with me or not, which was fine with me. The main issues they mentioned were the last three points of the second chart---human responsibility, evangelism and missions, and the necessity of the offer of the gospel to every person.

One young fellow, whom I didn't even know said, "Boy, until today I thought Calvinists were about as evil as Jack the Ripper. That's the way I have heard them presented." Of course, he was speaking with some hyperbolic language, but his statement had some truth to it.

Another young lady stopped by as she left and said, "This is the first time I have ever heard a clear and fair presentation of Calvinism. I too have been bombarded with a false and even dishonest caricature of Calvinism. I have always wondered how anyone could deny human responsibility, evangelism and missions, and the need to evangelize the world for Christ, when those truths are so clearly spelled out in the Bible. But that is what I was told Calvinists believed. But now I see such a view is a false representation of Calvinism! Why can't people be honest in dealing with these systems of theology?"

Chapter 33

The campus was a buzz over the noon meeting, and as expected, I received a phone call from Dr. Sisk and Dr. Welsh before the afternoon was over. Dr. Sisk said he was sorry he had not been able to attend, but had heard great things about it. Dr. Welsh was more cautious in what he stated, but he did seem grateful for the explanation. But he never said anything that indicated his previous involvement with any negativity on campus concerning the subject nor concerning Dink and me. On the whole I was very grateful for the way the Lord had blessed, and I was encouraged somewhat about the future.

Later that afternoon I heard from Daryl Sisk's lawyer and learned that they had let him out of jail on bond, partly because they were still trying to figure out what to do with him. He was told, however, that he could not leave the area. He gave me a phone number through his lawyer, where he would be staying in Minnesota, and so I called him in order to get the story first hand. He confirmed what the lawyer had said and that he had found a job and a place to stay, until the whole issue was settled. And he said that he and the girl were seeing each other. I warned him about that---not to let anything like what had taken place before even become a remote possibility!

After my five-minute or so lecture, he assured me that her mother had an eye on them also, and that was fine with them. He had introduced her to the Lord, and they were going to church together, which was one place her mother would let them go, even though her mother was not a Christian. He had not pressed her for any decision for Christ, as he wanted her to understand the gospel very clearly and the full meaning and implications of becoming a Christian. They were going to a church with a reformed perspective, and he said they were learning much about the truth of salvation and what it means to be a Christian. They were even going to Sunday School.

When we finished our conversation, I settled into my comfortable desk chair and spent a few moments thanking the Lord for the way He was working in so many areas. Matters were not settled in every situation, and several things could take a turn for the worse, but so far I knew I had much for which to praise Him! But, then, just when I was ready to head home about 4:00 PM, Dr. Sisk called and asked if I could come to his office immediately. I had no idea what was up, but I agreed to do so, but with some reservations! When I got there, I discovered that it was a meeting with Dr. Sisk and the Chairman of the Board of Trustees of the seminary, and I could sense the tension of the moment immediately, when I walked into the room.

Evidently, they had been discussing the gathering, which had taken place at the noon hour. I decided to let the Chairman of the Board do the talking, until I found out exactly what had brought him on campus so quickly, since he lived two hours away. He wanted to know why and how Dr. Sisk ever came to allow such a meeting on the campus at the noon hour?

Not wishing to be seen as out of order, and yet wanting to get him out of his ranting mode, I asked him what he was told had gone on at the meeting. He admitted that he didn't know exactly, but that Calvinism had been presented in full force at the meeting without any reply to it allowed. I asked him if he would be so gracious as to let me explain the whole situation to him before he drew any final conclusions. And though still upset, he agreed!

And so we spent the next two hours, which was interrupted only by a phone call to my wife to tell her I would be late for supper, talking about the whole setting on the campus. I told him that the situation had become explosive, mainly because of false rumors about Dink and me leaving the school. We were doing our best to subdue this uproar, which really was not of our making. I explained to him, that with Dr. Sisk's permission, we had called interested parties together for that noon meeting to explain some of the theological issues which were being batted around.

Then I went over my material with him (I had brought it with me with some suspicions that the meeting was for such a purpose), and I kept it just as objective as I did at the initial noon gathering. That he listened at first with some suspicion was obvious. But the further we went with it, the clearer it became that he was learning something from the material, as had the students. At the end of the presentation, I opened the floor again for questions and told him we would keep them objective, just as they were in the noon meeting.

By now the anger was gone, and he was like the students, as it was clear that he was learning something, whether he agreed with it or not, which is something I emphasized all through our discussion. We are here only to learn and to think, not just to agree or disagree on everything that is spoken. How can one ever refute correctly another view until he understands correctly what the view is stating? One might come to understand that this is the Biblical view.

When we were finished, I wasn't sure where he stood, but assumed that probably he still held the view he had, when he had come through the door. But at least, hopefully, the Lord had calmed him down some, and he could look at theological issues with more objectivity than previously. We prayed and then he left, thanking me for meeting with him. I didn't tell him anything further, except to wish him well, and that I hoped we could do this again sometime. And I meant it!

By the time I headed home that evening, it was dark outside, and I almost felt like I should be driving a fire truck, as I had been putting out fires all day! Spiritual arsonists seemed to be ruling the campus, as they crawled the halls of the school, and even extended as far as the seminary board members, faculty members, some students, and even administrative people. Only God knew really how far in all these areas. Gossip and rumors are like a prairie fire, as the wind carries various bits of burning brush near and far to light another tender branch or another dry piece of grass, and the fire spreads further and further.

As I drove, I prayed, "Lord, only you can put out this flame of gossip, which has engulfed this campus and beyond!" And then I thought, maybe there is another flame burning---the flame of the Lord for the cause of His truth!

Chapter 34

I didn't hear any more about this whole issue during the rest of the week. An eerie silence seemed to engulf the campus, at least concerning this subject. Perhaps, it had all gone underground and was being discussed in dorm rooms and at meals in the cafeteria and maybe even among other board members, who were getting the message through various sources. Sometimes the fire simmers getting even hotter before it breaks loose visibly once again.

Because of this uncertainty, it was with eagerness that I looked forward to meeting with Dr. Sisk once again, thinking maybe that we could learn of any further developments, good or bad, about the whole situation. Or maybe he would know some further news about Daryl. But when we met, nothing more was said on these subjects, so after prayer we turned to deal with our subject for the day.

I proceeded again by the statement of several thoughts in the further presentation of our subject.

1. There is no doubt about it that the Bible teaches salvation is by the grace of God alone, and all true Bible believers will agree with that statement, though they may disagree in their definition of what it means!

Ephesians 2:8-9
> *8 For by grace are ye saved through faith; and that not of yourselves: it is the gift of God: 9 Not of works, lest any man should boast.*

Titus 3:5
> *Not by works of righteousness which we have done, but according to his mercy he saved us, by the*

*washing of regeneration, and renewing of the Holy
Ghost.*

2. The question then becomes, is man saved by grace, if
   he himself has the ability to exercise faith in Christ for
   salvation in his own strength and power or would that
   be salvation by works?

   a. Arminians would say, yes, that God provides grace
      so that man is able to believe, if he wants to
      exercise faith, or he is able to reject Christ, if he so
      desires.   Either way the final determination of
      salvation is by the power and decision of man.

      It has at times been illustrated by a little boy passing
      by an orchard, yet he has no power to reach up into
      one of the trees and get himself an apple. But then
      a man comes by and lifts the little boy up, and now
      the little fellow can either reach out and take an
      apple, or he can refuse to take the apple and go on
      his way.

      This illustration is saying, when applied to faith and
      salvation, that God somehow neutralizes the effects
      of the fall. Some Arminians would say the effects
      of the fall were not too great to begin with, while
      others would see a more serious damage to man's
      being by the fall. Either way, God lifts every sinner
      up one way or another, and thereby every man can
      either say yes or no to Christ and salvation. It is all
      ultimately left up to man!

b. Calvinists would ask where this is taught clearly in Scripture. They would maintain that the effects of the fall are so great that man has lost his spiritual ability to desire or choose God. It is only by the grace of God that sinful men can be given the gift of faith in accordance with God's purpose and will in the choosing and saving of His elect, as noted previously in this study.

c. The question boils down, then, to what damage the fall brought to all mankind, and how are the effects of the fall overcome in the saving of a man by the grace of God. We are back to the question of monergism or synergism. Salvation must be monergistic, if the fall left a man in total depravity. Salvation is synergistic, if the effects of the fall are overcome or neutralized by some means, whereby man can then by his own power either choose or reject Christ and salvation.

3. The question then becomes, what effect did the fall have on man regarding any spiritual ability to cooperate with God in the work of salvation?

a. Ephesians 3:1
   You hath he quickened who <u>were dead</u> in trespasses and sin

   Surely, this refers to a spiritual death, and the quickening refers to God giving new spiritual life, as He saves us. It is not that God gives us ability, and then the choice is ours. It is that God gives us new life by regeneration, and the gifts of repentance and faith.

b. Romans 3:7-8

    10 there is none righteous, no, not one:
    11 there is none that understands
        (spiritual things)
    11 there is none that seeks after God.
    12 they are all gone out of the way
    12 they are together they have become
        unprofitable
    12 there is none that doeth good, no, not one.
    13 their throat is an open sepulcher
    13 with their tongues they have used deceit
    13 the poison of asps is under their lips
    14 whose mouth is full of cursing and
        bitterness:
    15 their feet are swift to shed blood:
    16 destruction and misery are in their ways:
    17 the way of peace have they not known:
    18 there is no fear of God before their eyes

c. Jeremiah 17:9

    *The heart is deceitful above all things, and
    desperately wicked: who can know it?*

The human heart is so wicked and deceitful that man cannot even know how wicked and deceitful his heart is. Someone needs to tell the Arminians this, for they see man's nature not too damaged by the fall, that is, not very wicked or deceitful. Does not the Arminian doctrine of man's ability show that Arminians do not know the wickedness and deceitfulness and inability of the human heart?

Is it not absolutely clear that
> All men are dead in sin!
> No man is righteous!
> No man understands the things of God!
> No man seeks after God!
> We are all in this condition!
> We are all unprofitable to God!
> Not one of us does any good!
> All our mouths are full of wickedness!
> We have not known the way of peace!
> Not one of us fears God!
> Remember that all of the above speaks of man
> > in his natural and unredeemed state!

d. Man is unworthy and God owes him nothing

Is it not true that when Adam sinned, all mankind became guilty before God?

> man is unworthy
> man is undeserving
> man is incapable in spiritual matters
> man deserves only hell and separation
> > from God forever
> man has no merit whereby he can obtain
> > grace or favor from God
> God would have been just to cast
> > us all immediately into hell
> > > because that was what we deserved
> man remains in that condition to this day

man's only hope is grace---
to be favored by God even though he
does not deserve it nor can he ever
deserve it
to be favored when we ought to be
in hell separated from God
is that not what grace is---unmerited favor?
clearly God owes man nothing
God is not responsible
to give man anything
to provide man a way out of his
predicament of sin
to allow man anything but justice---
which would be eternity in hell
man is unable to save himself by his works

e. But what if God to glorify and display His grace
determines to rescue some men from the power and
penalty of sin?

Is He obligated to save all? Is He unfair if He
chooses to save some and not all, according to His
will and purpose and grace?

Remember grace is unmerited favor---no man
deserves it! And if God chooses to show grace to
some and not all, when no one deserves anything to
begin with---how can that be unfair?

The marvel is not that God did not choose to save
everyone, but that He chose to save anyone at all
from such a fallen and wicked race! That is grace!

No man deserved anything but hell, but God by grace chose to save a people to glorify His grace---not man's worth, for man has no worth before God.

Since the fall, man is a fallen and wasted and undeserving sinner---except that he deserves only hell! Is this not what Scripture says clearly?

> *By grace are you saved through faith*
> *it is the gift of God*
> *it is not of works*
> *lest any man should boast*

Yes---that is the marvel of grace---
    that God chose to save a people
        who deserved nothing
        who had forfeited everything by sin
        who would never chose God
        who would never seek God on their own
        who would be rebels forever
            if God did not seek them
        who possessed nothing within themselves
            which would cause God to love them

The above is grace! Loving grace! Merciful grace! Sovereign grace! Pure grace with no mixture of man's works or ability! Why do men have trouble with that concept of true and pure grace? Do they not have trouble with such a doctrine because they want to see something in man as the basis of God's salvation, even something that obligates God to them?

But we must admit that grace is the motivating factor in the heart of God that causes God to save some men (remember He was not obligated to save any man). How we get it all turned around. We think He saves men because of something in the men! Or because of something we have done! Or because of something we could do! Or because of something we do first!

But the truth is that God saves men not because of who they are, and not because of what they have or can do or will do---for they can do nothing. God saves us not because of our ability to whip up a saving faith, for faith is the gift of God! No man is capable in his own strength or power to exercise faith in Jesus Christ, but rather God saves men for the praise of the glory of His grace and according to the good pleasure of His will (see Ephesians 1).

Clearly salvation is not about us, but salvation is about God---to glorify Him! To show and exalt His unmerited favor to sinners, who deserve nothing but eternity in hell! To save sinners, who by their own strength can do nothing to save themselves! To save sinners, who after they are saved can only say, "Look what God did! Look what I was without God's grace! Look where I would be for eternity except for His grace!"

Do we not understand what we are saying when we think or say, "I am the author of my faith! I had the power to exercise faith in my own strength! I chose God and Christ! I then acted by my power and was saved!" Isn't there a problem, if ones says, "I chose God because He saw I would choose Him!" Do not all of these statements give me the credit for my salvation or at least for being the final word concerning my salvation?

Do we realize what we are saying when we teach that God provides the way, but He can only wait for men to respond to His marvelous offer of grace and salvation? Does this not put God under my control and power? Does this not deny the sovereignty of God in all things, when we deny the sovereignty of God in salvation? He must wait upon me to make up my mind by my own will before He can save me! His hands are tied, until I decide to cooperate with him! Would any one ever be saved according to this doctrine, if we truly understood the doctrine of the depravity and helplessness of man in sin?

Our study time was up and our quitting time was even past due! I apologized for going overtime, but both Dr. Sisk and Dink said that they hadn't noticed the time, and they thanked me for the presentation. We did spend some further time discussing the thoughts of the day. But Dr. Sisk's secretary knew our time had expired, and like a good secretary, she reminded him of his next appointment. Thus, Dink and I were soon on our way.

When I got back to my office, after being flagged down by several students, who wanted to discuss the recent noon hour meeting, I found a stranger waiting for me. I had been trying to fly low below radar range on campus for those past several days, just for that very reason---so that students could think on the subject on their own and among themselves. The man waiting for me looked like a preacher, so I invited him into my office. Yet I couldn't help but wonder who he was, and what he wanted, and was he involved with the current doctrinal skirmish?

Chapter 35

When the gentleman was comfortably seated upon my couch at my invitation, he finally introduced himself. He was Rev. Johnny Rafferty, and he was pastor of the First Baptist Church of Lionsville, and further, he was a member of the seminary's board of trustees. He said he had been hearing about some of the discussions on campus, and he had heard that I was involved in the whole situation, and he wanted to ask me some questions about what was going on at the school.

He seemed like a very humble individual, and not one who was just trying to get information so he could be a gossip, or one who would stir up the brethren over the whole matter. But a person cannot be too sure at such times as this. One can appear to be something they are not, just to get information that you would not ordinarily give to them. There is always a possibility that they might take it and use it to create havoc and division. And many times on such occasions, they would even twist what you had shared with them, for theirs or someone else's purpose. So I decided I had better be cautious in dealing with him.

"Yes, sir, we have been having some discussions concerning the sovereignty of God on campus, and, I think that they have been very profitable!" I informed him.

"Well, forgive me for my further questions," he stated, almost apologetically, "but I would like to know why you are teaching and promoting this doctrine called the sovereignty of God in our Baptist schools. Some also call it Calvinism or the doctrines of grace. Now I know I am a little older than you are, but in the Baptist churches I grew up in nothing of that sort was ever mentioned or preached.

"I was a businessman before I surrendered to preach several years ago, and I made a good bit of money. Some would say that I am independently wealthy. I guess that's why I am on the board of the seminary!" he said with a smile. "I say that so you will understand that I never had much opportunity for schooling. So, this thing called Calvinism is all new to me, and it just doesn't seem to be Baptistic, because I never heard it preached in our denomination's churches until just a few years ago. And now it's everywhere! I thought maybe you could explain to me why such doctrines are being used now to hijack our churches and denomination, when such theology was unknown in our churches in the earlier part of the twentieth century? And besides, isn't that Presbyterian doctrine, and if so, what is it doing in our Baptist churches?"

I really didn't detect any sharpness in his voice, as he was asking the question, but there were several words that could have been looked upon as inflammatory, such as "hijack" and the accusation of "Presbyterian doctrine," when speaking of Baptists. So I smiled back at him and asked him how much time he had! Did he want the full answer, which could take us several hours or more, or the reader's digest version?

"Well, if you have the time, can you make it somewhere in between the two choices you gave me?" he said with a friendly laugh.

So, I pulled down my book of Baptist confessions and began turning to certain pages, asking him to read various sections of different confessions, as I gave some explanation of the confession concerning its date and place of origin, along with some facts of the historical setting.

I thought he might have a heart attack by the look that came over his face as he continued reading!

Chapter 36

When he had finished reading all the sections from the different confessions, he was still shocked!

"I didn't realize Baptists ever believed anything like this! I was reared from childhood in one of our Baptist churches! And you said that those two confessions you showed me, the Second London Confession of 1689 and the Philadelphia Confession of 1742, are copies of the Westminster Confession of Faith for the most part? I was always told that Baptists were not and had never been a confessional people and that all we needed was the Bible!"

"Well, there is a measure of truth to that!" I replied. "Baptists do see the Bible as the highest authority, and that all things must be judged by Scripture. We do not use these confessions to judge the Bible, but we would judge all beliefs and confessions by the Bible. But this does not mean that we have not and should not make use of confessions of faith. True, we must be careful not to allow a confession equal authority or greater authority than Scripture! But Baptists of days gone by in their post-reformation history used confessions to explain what they believed and to give to the lay people a better understanding of doctrine."

"Well, when and why did Baptists quit using those confessions that I just read?" he asked again.

"This is where I might have to give you the reader digest version. Baptists held faithfully to these doctrines in the early part of the 1700's and even through that century with the coming of the First Great Awakening. In fact that awakening had a Calvinistic foundation, as it was based on the theology of such men as Jonathan Edwards and George Whitefield, who were not Baptists, but held to reformation doctrine. But Baptists did not participate initially in that movement of God.

"Yet, Baptists were eventually impacted by the results of the first great awakening, as the eighteenth century unfolded, as many of the converts of that awakening left the established churches of the day and joined Baptist churches. And of course, many of these people were not grounded in doctrine, and were more experiential than they were doctrinal, and in time they brought that kind of an influence to Baptists, good or bad.

"In the passing of the years and on into the 19th century, and even through the second great awakening of that century, Baptists were further influenced by a broader theology, including the impact of Charles G. Finney. He claimed to be a Presbyterian, but later admitted that he had never read the Westminster Confession of Faith (see William G. McLoughlin, *Modern Revivalism: Charles Grandison Finney to Billy Graham*, New York: The Ronald Press, 1959, p. 23). Slowly through that century and on into the twentieth century, the emphasis for Baptists became evangelism and more evangelism with a continual diminishing of the need and importance of their historical doctrine as a foundation for true evangelism. By the middle of the twentieth century, Baptists in most places had all but jettisoned their Calvinistic theological basis in favor of a shallow understanding of doctrine, which favored an evangelism at any price, even if it meant the addition to their churches of false fruit and shallow living.

"Many of us, you and I no doubt included, were influenced by this brand of Baptist theology, which had no understanding of past history or of the great historical confessions of faith. And, we were shocked, when we first heard of the revival of Calvinism in our day, as that doctrine began to be preached again among Baptists, who were only returning to their historical roots and confessions of faith. We thought, as you put it, that someone was 'hijacking' our denomination to take us down a road over which Baptists had never traveled before, when in reality it was just a return to our historical and theological roots.

"Yet in the passing of time, I don't know about you, but I came to understand the damage which Arminian theology had done to Baptists! It had not only robbed us of our theology and separated us from our roots, but it had also filled our churches with many lost people, because of the practice of a false and shallow evangelism, which majored on an Arminian methodology, which was consistent with the new Arminian theology. Numbers and decisions and large church memberships became the mark of a great preacher and church, which thinking perverted the message and methodology and the ministry even more.

"With the passing of the years, church impurity among Baptists became the hallmark of our churches, as lost people flooded the ranks, and no one dared hold them accountable for their loose lives and questionable living. No one dared question anyone else's profession of faith, even if that questionable person was living like a heretic or an apostate or a libertine. Lost men became not only members of our churches, but eventually were leaders in our churches in the ministry and in other positions of importance. If a preacher did come into such a church and try to preach the gospel and establish Biblical standards and historical Baptist doctrine, he was soon dismissed as a troublemaker and church-divider, and not a Baptist.

"Thus, Brother Rafferty, though some of us didn't know it, because we had been prejudiced against Calvinism, we were ready for the truth which was found in that system of thought. But we didn't know we were ready until we came to a true understanding of Calvinism or the doctrines of grace. We had several layers of falsehood to peal away from the term 'Calvinism' before we knew what that doctrine really taught. We had been told that Calvinism made God unfair, that it would kill evangelism and missions, that it was not Baptistic, that it robbed man of his free will, that it dehumnized man, that it made him a robot or an automaton, etc, and etc.

"Now I can't speak for anyone else, but I think my testimony has been repeated by many others. When I understood what Calvinism really was, and it had been explained to me from Scripture, I not only embraced it as the truth, but I also saw the great importance of it for the church today, as it was for Baptists in the past!"

I had watched his face as I spoke, and I could tell he was giving this subject some deep thought. I hadn't intended to go on that long without his response, but there was no place for me to break before giving something of a complete but condensed presentation of the subject.

When he finally spoke, there was a deep sincerity in his voice, as he said, "Dr. Pointer, I want to thank you for taking your time to explain all this to me! I was like a man lost in a storm at sea in trying to understand what this furor was all about, until I heard your explanation! When I had questions about this subject, I got all kinds of answers, but never something as clear as your explanation!"

He never said whether or not he agreed with my viewpoint, but that was not the issue. He had come to an understanding of the subject, rather than having just a knee-jerk emotional reaction to it. I had told him if he thought about the matter further, and he wanted to talk again to let me know. For this he seemed to be grateful!

Chapter 37

Things calmed down after the events of the week just described, and before we knew it, Monday was upon us again. I decided that I would use the material in the Monday meeting with Dr. Sisk that I had used in the discussion with Pastor Johnny Rafferty. I ran off copies of it for Dink and Dr. Sisk to follow, as I gave an introduction and then the statement of the confession, followed by a brief summary. In our meeting we simply went through the material. I gave only chosen statements from the Second London Baptist Confession, and none from the Philadelphia Confession, because the latter was a copy of the former.

I noted for them further that the Second London Confession of Faith of 1689 was the Particular Baptist confession of faith. There were two groups of Baptists in their early history in England, the General Baptists and the Particular Baptists. The Particular Baptists became the prominent group of Baptists, as the General Baptists faded almost from the scene. It was again, for the most part, that Baptists in America were of the Particular Baptist group, as evidenced in the Philadelphia Confession of Faith, as they so strongly mirrored the Particular Baptists in England. The Southern Baptist Encyclopedia calls the Philadelphia Baptist Confession the Baptist confession of faith of the early Baptists in America. Anyone who knows his Baptist history knows also that Southern Baptists in their early days also held strong Calvinistic convictions.

**EXCERPTS FROM THE SECOND LONDON
CONFESSION OF FAITH OF 1689
(The Confessional Statement Is Given First
Followed by a Brief Summary)**

Chapter 3: Of God's Decree

1. God hath decreed in himself, from all eternity, by the
   most wise and holy counsel of his own will, freely and
   unchangeably, all things, whatsoever comes to pass; yet
   so as thereby is God neither the author of sin nor hath
   fellowship with any therein; nor is violence offered to
   the will of the creature, nor yet is the liberty or
   contingency of second causes taken away, but rather
   established; in which appears his wisdom in disposing
   all things, and power and faithfulness in accomplishing
   his decree.

   > God has decreed whatever comes to pass
   >   but He is not the author of sin
   >   and no violence is offered to man's will
   >   (violence meaning force).
   > This does not rule out second causes.

2. Although God knoweth whatsoever may or can come to
   pass, upon all supposed conditions, yet hath he not
   decreed anything, because he foresaw it as future, or as
   that which would come to pass upon such conditions.

   > God has not decreed anything on the basis
   >   of foreknowledge---that is because He saw it
   >   as future or as that which would come
   >   to pass based on certain conditions.

3. By the decree of God, for the manifestation of his glory,
   some men and angels are predestinated, or foreordained
   to eternal life through Jesus Christ, to the praise of his
   glorious grace; others being left to act in their sin to

their just condemnation, to the praise of his glorious justice.

> God has decreed some men and angels
> to eternal life through Jesus Christ
> to the praise of His glorious grace
> and for the manifestation of His glory.
> God has left others to act in their sin
> to their just condemnation also for the praise
> of His glorious justice.

4. These angels and men thus predestinated and foreordained, are particularly and unchangeably designed, and their number so certain and definite, that it cannot be either increased or diminished.

> These men and angels are predestinated
> and foreordained and particularly and
> unchangeably designed so that their number
> is so certain and definite that it cannot be
> either increased or diminished.

5. Those of mankind that are predestinated to life, God, before the foundation of the world was laid, according to his eternal and immutable purpose, and the secret counsel and good pleasure of his will, hath chosen in Christ unto everlasting glory, out of his mere free grace and love, without any other thing in the creature as a condition or cause moving him thereunto.

> Those men who are predestinated to life by God
> before the foundation of the world according
> to His eternal and immutable purpose

and the secret counsel and His pleasure
He has chosen in Christ
unto everlasting glory
by His free grace and love
without any condition
or cause found
in the creature.

Chapter 9: Of Free Will

1. God hath endued the will of man with that natural liberty and power of acting upon choice, that it is neither forced, nor by any necessity of nature determined to do good or evil.

   God has given man a will with liberty
   and power of choice that is neither forced
   nor by any necessity of nature determined
   to do good or evil.
   This seems to be speaking of man's initial state
   of creation before the fall.
   (see the following statements)

2. Man, in his state of innocency, had freedom and power to will and to do that which was good and well-pleasing to God, yet was unstable, so that he might fall from it.

   Man in his state of innocency (before the fall)
   did have freedom and power to will and to do
   that which was good and pleasing to God
   but yet man was unstable so that
   he might fall from that state into sin.

3. Man, by his fall into a state of sin, hath wholly lost all
    ability of will to any spiritual good accompanying
    salvation; so as a natural man, being altogether averse
    from that good, and dead in sin, is not able by his own
    strength to convert himself, or to prepare himself
    thereunto.

> Man fell into a state of sin and has wholly lost
>   all ability of his will to do any spiritual good
>   which accompanies salvation.
> Thus man as a natural man is altogether averse
>   from that spiritual good and is dead in sin
>   and therefore has no ability
>   by his own strength to convert himself
>   or to prepare himself
>   for his conversion.

4. When God converts a sinner, and translates him into the
    state of grace, he freeth him from his natural bondage
    under sin, and by his grace alone enables him freely to
    will and to do that which is spiritually good; yet so as
    that by reason of his remaining corruptions, he doth not
    perfectly, nor only will, that which is good, but doth
    also will that which is evil.

> When God saves a sinner and translates him
>   into the state of grace He frees him
>   from his natural bondage under sin
>   and by His grace alone enables him
>   freely to will and to do
>   that which is spiritually good
>   but he is not perfect.

5. This will of man is made perfectly and immutably free to good alone in the state of glory only.

> The will of man is only made perfectly
> and immutably free to do good alone
> in the state of glory (or eternity).

Chapter 10: Of Effectual Calling

1. Those whom God hath predestinated unto life, he is pleased in his appointed, and accepted time, effectually to call, by his Word and Spirit, out of that state of sin and death in which they are by nature, to grace and salvation by Jesus Christ; enlightening their minds spiritually and savingly to understand the things of God; taking away their heart of stone, and giving unto them a heart of flesh; renewing their wills, and by his almighty power determining them to that which is good, and effectually drawing them to Jesus Christ; yet so as they come most freely, being made willing by his grace.

> God effectually calls out of the state
> of sin and death in His appointed time
> by His Word and Spirit those He has
> predestinated unto life.
> God effectually calls them to grace and
> salvation in Jesus Christ---enlightening
> their minds spiritually and savingly
> so that they understand
> the things of God.
> God takes away their heart of stone
> and gives them a heart of flesh.

God renews their wills and by His almighty power.
   determines them to that which is good.
      and effectually draws them to Jesus Christ
         yet they come most freely
            being made willing by His grace.

2. This effectual call is of God's free and special grace alone, not from anything at all foreseen in man, nor from any power or agency in the creature, being wholly passive therein, being dead in sins and trespasses, until being quickened and renewed by the Holy Spirit; he is thereby enabled to answer this call, and to embrace the grace offered and conveyed in it, and that by no less power than that which raised up Christ from the dead.

This effectual call is of God's free grace
   and special grace alone.
It is not from anything at all forseen in man---
   nor from any power or agency in the creature
      man being wholly passive therein
         and being dead in sins and trespasses
            until he is quickened and renewed
               by the Holy Spirit.
Man is thereby enabled by God's free grace
   to answer God's effectual call and to embrace
      the grace offered and conveyed in the call
         and also by no less power
            which raised up Christ from the dead.

When we had finished going over this material, we had just enough time for some lively discussion. Dr. Sisk himself seemed surprised at the clarity of the doctrine of the Calvinistic position in those confessional statements.

Whether one agreed with the statements or not, one had to admit that the introduction of Calvinistic doctrine into a Baptist seminary was not any "hijacking" of historical Baptist thinking. In fact, one could make the case that Baptist thinking had been hijacked earlier in its history by Arminian thoughts and tendencies, and it was only the ignorance of Baptist history that made one think the opposite!

Before we left Dr. Sisk shared with us some news, that Daryl was soon to be out of jail and on his way home. He had gotten off with a fine, a rather large one, and Dr. Sisk was going to pay it, and Daryl would pay him back over the years. And, perhaps even more encouraging, was the news that he and the girl had come to the decision of the necessity of a parting of their ways.

Daryl had admitted that he had sensed an obligation towards her, in light of all that she had been through, but even though the girl was now a Christian, as they both had prayed about it, they came to the conclusion that it was not God's will. She would be going to a Christian college, as the next step in God's will for her life, and Daryl would be returning home. Maybe someday, but now was not the time. They agreed that each one needed time to seek His will for their lives. He must come first!

I had to admit that I was greatly encouraged, as was Dink, to hear these things, as it showed real maturity concerning their future lives for Christ. Surely this must be the attitude of every Christian! God and His will must come first, and then we can make all other decisions in life, including marriage!

Chapter 38

I felt somewhat relieved as I walked back to my office. One of the issues of the semester was settled, as Daryl would soon be on his way home, out of his legal trouble, and he was also settled in his plans for the future---to put the Lord first and do His will. But the other matter was still hanging over our heads---our future at the seminary! And all was because of a doctrine, which Baptists had held firmly in their early history, but also a doctrine of which many modern day Baptists were totally ignorant. I didn't realize how soon this issue would be pushed to the front of the current problem once again.

It began with another visitor at my office later in the afternoon, as I was getting ready for the next day's classes. I instinctively invited someone in when I heard a knock on my door, and I noted when the door opened that my visitor was a stranger to me.

"Dr. Pointer?" the voice said in a demanding manner, as if the speaker was upset with me.

I kindly replied yes, and invited him to come on in, and he immediately teed off on me, not even giving us an opportunity to get acquainted with one another.

"Dr. Pointer, you don't know me, but I have heard a lot about you, and I have concluded that you are not one of us!" he stated adamantly.

"Not 'one of us'?" I asked with some bewilderment. "Who is the 'us' that you are referring to in your accusation?"

"You are not a Baptist nor an Evangelistic Baptist!" he stated authoritatively. For the reader's benefit, our denomination was known as the Evangelistic Baptist Convention.

"I really do not understand how you were ever hired to teach at one of our denominational schools!" he stated his convictions firmly once again.

"Well, I went to our denomination's schools, college and seminary, all the way to a doctorate! Doesn't that make me 'one of us'?" I said, leading him on.

"No, not necessarily!" he responded sharply.

"Well, I have pastored several denominational churches over the years, and I have preached in dozens of other denominational churches during that same time frame! Doesn't that make me 'one of us'?" I asked him again.

"No, not at all!" he affirmed curtly.

"Then, let me try again!" I offered. "I believe in the Bible as the divinely inspired Word of God! Doesn't that make me 'one of us'?" I tried again.

"No, no, no, no!" he almost shouted.

"All the churches I ever pastored gave to the denominational missions program! Does that help?" I queried with a smile, and I think he got it by now that I was being sarcastic with him for his empty accusation. But I added quickly, before he could shout at me again, "If none or all of the above does not make me 'one of us', I guess I will never be 'one of us,' whoever 'us' might be!"

Then I must admit that I got quite sarcastic with him, when I said, "I have never heard of the 'ONE OF US Baptist Convention. Maybe you can tell me about it!"

With that I gave him the floor, and I found out, as expected, that he was another of those like Pastor Johnny Rafferty, only he had an entirely different attitude than Pastor Rafferty. He wasn't here to learn anything, because he knew it all already. He was another one who thought I was one of those robber-barons who was hijacking his precious denomination by believing the doctrines of

Calvinism. He was so flustered by now, that he could only stand and stammer. So I took the floor once again.

"Sir, do you believe the doctrine of the priesthood of every believer?" I said, knowing I had him on this one, because if he was typical of others I had met like him, that was the doctrine they hid behind, when they were propagating false doctrine. Grudgingly, he answered yes!

"Well, then can you define that doctrine for me!" I asked once again.

"Uh, it means that a Baptist will not have his conscience bound by any man or any doctrine---no one can tell a Baptist what to believe!" he offered.

I didn't agree with that statement or definition of the doctrine, but by defining it that way he had walked right into my trap.

"Then how can you come in here and tell me I am not an Evangelistic Baptist because I am not 'one of us' or 'one of your group' or whoever you are talking about? Aren't you seeking to bind my conscience to whatever doctrine it is that is bothering you today, which you believe but I do not?"

"Well, there are certain things we as Baptists do believe and don't believe!" he tried again.

"Then you don't believe in the doctrine of the priesthood of the believer, according to your definition of that doctrine. So which is it? Do you believe that doctrine or don't you believe that doctrine? You don't seem to be too sure of what you do or don't believe, and it seems to me you had better get that straightened out before you come and accuse me of not being an Evangelistic Baptist!"

With that he headed for the door, as I was still speaking and saying, "Sir, I didn't even get your name!" All I heard after that was the slamming of my office door!

Chapter 39

I must admit I was a little bit perturbed by the accusations of my previous visitor. I guess I should have been use to it by now, since I had faced such false thinking so many times previously. But all the build-up around the problem at the seminary had gotten to me. It wasn't long until I got a call from Dr. Sisk!

"Dr. Pointer! Did you just talk a little while ago with Pastor Larry Hollister?" he asked.

I laughed, as I said, "I talked with someone who stormed in here like a hurricane and accused me of not being 'one of us,'" and I played along with him, trying to find out who 'us' was! But he never could or would answer my question or give his name!"

"Well, that was Larry Hollister, and he's in my office now and is very offended. Can you come over and smooth this out?" he requested.

"I will be glad to come over, but I am not sure we can straighten it out. Ask him what went on, and then I will give you my perspective, when I get there!" I suggested.

As I walked to Dr. Sisk's office, I really didn't know what to expect, and, honestly, I wondered what good it was going to do to meet with him again, unless his attitude had changed. He was a man who was a little older than I was, about the age of Pastor Rafferty, and I began to get the suspicion that he had come because of a conversation with Brother Rafferty. I couldn't believe that he could have been sent by anyone, especially Pastor Rafferty.

When I walked into Dr. Sisk's office, I could almost see the steam still coming out of Larry Hollister's ears! His eyes were glassy, his brow was still furrowed, and his first words had not changed one bit. He seemed to me like a little boy who thought he could get me in trouble by running and telling my mommy on me (mother in this case being Dr. Sisk, the president of the seminary).

"Dr. Sisk!" he began, while he pointed at me, "This is the man who showed me no respect, as I was only there trying to help him!"

With painful grace and kindness, and a smile, which I hoped he wouldn't misinterpret, I said, "Sir, I beg to differ with you. You were not there to help me, but you were there to censure me for my beliefs and exclude me from my denominational affiliation, at least in your mind and by your accusations. I was only seeking to defend myself, even at times with some humor and comical sarcasm, which I am sure you didn't appreciate, because it exposed your purpose and the weakness of your arguments and position. You must admit that you jumped on me without even giving me your name and without letting me get acquainted with you, when I had never met you before. You wanted to put me on the defensive, and now you are upset because I defended myself and put you on the defensive instead!"

When he tried to speak again, he was almost speechless, so I suggested, "Why don't we start all over? I am Ira Pointer and now I know you are Larry Hollister! And we have Dr. Sisk here to referee, if need be. Now, what was it that you wanted to talk to me about?"

But instead of seizing the moment, and moving on to have a sane discussion of whatever he wanted to say, he seemed to want to pout about the whole thing.

"Well, I just can't understand, how you can treat a member of the seminary board of trustees the way you treated me! It's unheard of in denominational circles to act that way to one's superiors!" he continued.

I wondered if his pride had caused him to think that his position allowed him to insult those he thought were his inferiors. Maybe that had been his practice in his experience in denominational politics! Now he thought that a mere professor should cower before him in fear and trembling, allowing him to say to me whatever he wanted without me ever saying anything in return, just because he was a noble member of the seminary board. I surely didn't expect any such attitude from him toward me, and I was willing to give him his due respect, if he would only allow me. I was not going to grovel before him, as if I was in the wrong in the whole situation.

And then he did what one could have expected from such a man. He threatened me as he said, "And to think that I and the other members of the board, my close associates, will determine whether or not you stay at this seminary! How dare you treat me in this manner!"

I smiled, as I said, "Don't you remember what Jesus said to Pilate? 'You have no power over me, except it be given you by the Father!' I say the same thing to you and your friends on the board. It is not that I disrespect any of the board members, including you, nor your positions. But your threats are unchristian and even ungodly, and will come to fruition only in accordance with God's purpose and will. Personally, I would not like to be in your shoes in the future!"

I noticed that Dr. Sisk gulped at that statement, and his eyes got almost as big as saucers. He suggested that we pray, which he did, as Larry Hollister got up and walked out of the room, slamming the door once again.

Dr. Sisk just stood there and shook his head, and then he said, "It's going to take a miracle to keep you here now!"

Chapter 40

When I got back to my office, I called Dink. He answered with his usual friendly greeting, when he asked, "What's up, Preacha!"

"Well, Dink, I may have jumped from the frying pan into the fire today, as far as the seminary is concerned, and I took you with me!"

But it didn't seem to bother him, as he replied, "Dat's okay, Preacha! We'se been der before, ain't we? But tell me 'bout it anyway!"

After explaining the whole situation to him, we had prayer, committing our future to the Lord, and then I left for home! It would be good to sit in my easy chair with no office door to open to strangers or students or anyone else. I felt like I could sit there and vegetate for the rest of the evening. So after explaining it all to Terry, my wife, and then after supper with the kids, I headed for that chair, and was soon practicing some toes up meditation---until the phone rang! It was Dr. Sisk!

"I just thought I needed to tell you that Larry Hollister is calling for a special board meeting this coming Saturday to deal with your and Dink's situation, and the Executive Board has approved it!" he informed me.

"It didn't take him long, did it?" I answered.

"What do you think I should do?" he asked me.

"Nothing, except pray!" I answered.

"You don't think I should call any of the board members to explain to them what happened, and why Larry is so out of joint over this whole matter?" he asked.

I was sure Larry Hollister had been and would be doing some politicking concerning the matter, but I was surprised that Dr. Sisk thought that maybe we ought to do some.

"No, sir! I think we can plan what we want to present at the board meeting, but I don't think it would be right to go out and politic the issues like a bunch of worldlings. If God can't take care of it, what good would it do for Christian people to adopt worldly practices to do the Lord's work? There's too much of that already!"

Dr. Sisk did agree with me on second thought, and he thanked me for my spirit concerning the whole matter. I was then free to return to my vegatating, while I drifted in and out of consciousness. I had learned from the past that it was far better to let the mind relax, while one was mulling over a situation, than try to stay awake and figure out an answer. I couldn't count the times, when I dozed off thinking and praying about a matter, only to wake up with the answer, and I had to admit the answer was of the Lord! And maybe He would do it again! And He did!

I came to the conclusion that Dink and I would ask for a listing of the accusations, which were going to be brought against us. Surely, if this meeting concerned our future at the seminary, we would also ask and expect to receive several hours of time to address the board of trustees concerning our doctrines also. I immediately called Dr. Sisk back, and he was convinced that the board had to and would agree with our requests concerning the meeting.

But then I had one more question for Dr. Sisk.

"What are we going to do if this meeting gets out to the student body?" I asked. "Have the trustees thought of that, or are they even aware that could be a problem?"

"That's a good question!" he answered! "Let me talk with the executive board members, and get back to you!"

And then the phone rang again! It was a student, who already knew about the meeting! Nothing travels as fast as gossip---not even light! May the Lord help us!

Chapter 41

Dink and I were certainly busy the rest of that week, gearing up for the Saturday meeting. The executive board had agreed to give us time to present our case, and so we worked on our outline, so that we would be ready. I would present half of it and Dink the other half, just so they wouldn't think the beliefs were only mine or that Dink was just a dupe in the whole situation. That had already been stated by a few, as a reason he didn't belong as a teacher at a seminary, but that had not been stated by the students.

The student body did come alive during the week over this issue, and I almost had to tie several of my students down to keep them from doing something. But at this point, whatever anyone did would be out of place and counter productive. Let the matter take its course, and see what the Lord would do. Finally Saturday arrived.

The meeting opened with a semblance of prayer, and then the accusations were presented by none other than Larry Hollister himself. They were the usual flimsy and false accusations that are brought against Calvinists. We were accused of believing that cursed doctrine, which denies man his free will, makes God unfair, kills evangelism, denies Baptist doctrine, etc. and etc. As soon as I heard the first few items, I smiled to myself, and thought that these accusations were exactly what we had been studying, which meant our defense would answer every false statement that would be made about us.

The ones accusing us were so confident that their little arguments were fatal to us, that they turned it over to us after only about fifteen minutes of their assault against us. It was then that I passed out our document, which set forth the content of the following outline.

OUTLINE OF STUDY
(The chapters listed below
refer to the chapters of this book)

I THE SOVEREIGNTY OF GOD SHOWN TO BE SCRIPTURAL (Chapter 5)

A. The Verses Listed

Ephesians 1:11	Psalm 33:22	
Psalm 115:3	Daniel 4:35	
Proverbs 8:15	Proverbs 21:1	
Isaiah 14:27	Proverbs 19:21	
Psalm 76:10	Acts 2:23	Acts 4:27-28

B. What these verses teach us

God's decree concerns everything
    that comes to pass in my life
God's decree does not allow any chance-happenings
    or accidents to come into my life
God's decree extends to all events and creatures
    in the world as well as to me
God's decree extends to all history of the nations
    and all the events therein
God's decree extends to every aspect of every life
    including the life and actions
        of every believer
    including the life and actions of every lost man
        and every wicked deed
God's decree does not make God the author of sin

II THE SOVEREIGNTY OF GOD AND THE WILL OF MAN AND THE RESULTING DOCTRINAL RAMIFICATIONS (Chapter 7)

A. Is God's decree based on foreordination or foreknowledge?

B. Is God sovereign over all things except the will of man?

C. If God is sovereign over all things except the will of man, does this not make one an Arminian?

III THE SOVEREIGNTY OF GOD AND THE WILL OF MAN ACCORDING TO THE ARMINIAN AND THE CALVINIST (Chapter 8)

A. The effect of the fall on man's will according to the Calvinist

B. The effect of the fall on man's will according to the Arminian

C. The grace of God in salvation according to the Calvinist and Arminian---
    a. prevenient grace or irresistible grace?
    b. irresistible grace---does God force a man to be saved?

IV THE SOVEREIGNTY OF GOD IN RELATIONSHIP TO THE WICKED DEEDS OF MEN---IS GOD THE AUTHOR OF SIN? (Chapter 11)

A. Acts 2:23

B. Acts 4:27-28

C. God's sovereignty and the responsibility of man

V THE SOVEREIGNTY OF GOD IS LOST IF MAN IS SOVEREIGN OVER ONE AREA OF HIS LIFE (Chapter 14)

A. If God is not sovereign over all things, then He becomes a reactionary to someone else and their actions, which means He is not sovereign over all things

B. If man is sovereign over one area of his own life, then God is not sovereign

C. The will of man is not sovereign over one event of his own life, yet he is still a responsible creature before God

D. The proper definition of man's freedom and man's lack of freedom

E. Monergism and synergism in the salvation of a man---which is it?

VI THE SOVEREIGNTY OF GOD AND THE DOCTRINE OF ELECTION ACCORDING TO ROMANS 9 AND THE QUESTION REGARDING THE CLAIM THAT SUCH A DOCTRINE RELIEVES MAN OF HIS RESPONSIBILITY AND ACCOUNTABILITY BEFORE GOD (Chapters 17 AND 19)

A. Chapter 17---The proper definition of election (Romans 9:1-13)
  1. The true Israel is denunciated Scripturally 1-8
     a. *The true Israel is not fleshly Israel 1-5*
     b. *The true Israel is the spiritual Israel   6-8*
  2. The true Israel is entered sovereignly   9-13
     a. *The basis of election is clearly stated   9-11*
     b. *The example of election is clear also 11-13*
  3. The summary of the matter
     a. *The true Israel of God includes both Jews and Gentiles*
     b. *The true Israel of God was elected by God.*
     c. *The true Israel of God is given new life by the power of God*

B. Chapter 19---The powerful defense of election--- Romans 9:14-23
  1. Objection One
     a. *Stated   14*
        What shall we say? Is there unrighteousness with God?
     b. *Objection One Answered   15-18*
  2. Objection Two   19-23
     a. *Objection Two Stated   19*
        Then wilt thou say unto me, Why doth He yet find fault? For who has resisted His will?
     b. *Objection Two Answered   20*
        1). A bold statement   20
           Nay but O man, who are you that replies against God?
        2). A convincing illustration   20
           The potter and the vessel

3. Conclusion   24-33
    a. The effectual call to salvation has come to Jews and Gentiles 24
    b. This inclusion of Jews and Gentiles in the true Israel of God was prophesied by Hosea and agreed upon by Isaiah 25-27
    c. God will perform His Word on earth 28
    d. What can we say then?

VIII THE SOVEREIGNTY OF GOD THOUGH RENDERING MAN TO BE A RESPONSIBLE CREATURE DOES NOT MEAN THAT MAN IS ABLE TO DO WHAT GOD REQUIRES AND COMMANDS HIM TO DO (Chapter 21)

A. Are all men responsible to keep the Ten Commandments with perfection though they are not able?---Yes!

B. Are all men responsible to repent and believe the Gospel though they are not able?---Yes

C. An illustration---Matthew 13:1-13---The man with a withered arm

IX THE SOVEREIGNTY OF GOD AS A BASIS FOR PRAYER ACCORDING TO THE CALVINIST AND THE ARMINIAN (Chapter 23)

A. The Arminian has no solid basis for prayer
B. The Calvinist does have the solid basis for prayer

X   THE SOVEREIGNTY OF GOD AS A BASIS FOR EVANGELISM AND MISSIONS ACCORDING TO THE CALVINIST AND THE ARMINIAN (Chapter 25)

A. No church or Christian should authorize any kind of an evangelistic approach or missions program on the basis of pragmatism---that is the idea that the best program and approach is the one that gets the most decisions or results or builds the biggest church---we must and can depend on the power of God

B. The Calvinist has a far different motivation and basis for engaging in the work of evangelism and missions---God is calling out His elect through that work

XI THE SOVEREIGNTY OF GOD AND THE EFFECTUAL CALL TO SALVATION (Chapter 27)

A. What About John 10?
   1. That there are many false shepherds!
   2. That there is one true shepherd (the Lord Jesus Himself)!
   3. That the doorkeeper of the sheepfold opens the door of the sheepfold to the true shepherd!
   4. That the true shepherd comes into the sheepfold and calls out His sheep!
   5. That the true sheep and only the true sheep (God's elect) hear the voice or call of the true shepherd!

6. That the true sheep will not (emphatic negative in the Greek language) follow the voice or call of a stranger!

7. That the true sheep will flee from the voice of a stranger, because they know it is not the voice of the true shepherd!

8. That this is speaking of the effectual call of God to His elect for their salvation!

9. That those who heard this parable of Christ did not understand what He was saying, and should it not be any surprise to us when men do not understand these doctrines today?

B. I Corinthians 1:18-31

1. The preaching of the cross is to them that are perishing foolishness!   18

2. The preaching of the cross is the power of God to us who are saved!   18

3. The wisdom of man is powerless in this work of salvation!   19

4. The wisdom of man is foolishness to God!   20

5. The world by wisdom does not know God!   20

6. It pleases God by the foolishness of preaching to save them that believe!   21

7. Men are impressed more by other means than by the preaching of a cross---the Jews require a sign and the Greeks seek after wisdom!   22

8. But Paul preaches Christ crucified, which he admits is to the Jews a stumblingblock and to the Greeks foolishness!   23

9. But unto <u>them who are called</u>, both Jews and Gentiles, Christ is the power of God and the wisdom of God---it is the effectual call of God that makes the difference!   23

10. For you see your <u>calling</u>, brethren, how that not many wise men after the flesh (are called), not many mighty men (are called), not many noble men (are called)!   26

11. But God has chosen the foolish things of the world to confound the wise, and God has chosen the weak things of the world to confound the mighty, and God has chosen the base things of the world, and things that are despised, yea, even things which are not, to bring to NOTHING the things that are! 27-28

12. And why has God chosen such people? So that no flesh should glory in His presence. So that we all would acknowledge that we are what we are because God has made unto us wisdom and righteousness and sanctification and redemption through Christ Jesus! 29-30

13. So if we glory, we will glory in the Lord!   31

Can it be denied that these verses speak of an effectual call to salvation?

XII THE SOVEREIGNTY OF GOD AND CHRIST'S PARTICULAR DEATH FOR HIS SHEEP (Chapter 29)

See John 10:11, 14-15, 17-18

> Do not these verses in John 10 make it very clear that Christ was in control of His death in every aspect, including the purpose for which He died? for His sheep (His elect or chosen ones)! He rose for His sheep! He knows His sheep and they know Him! He does all of this of His own accord and for a purpose---the purpose for which His Father sent Him to this earth---to save a people!

See Ephesians 5:25

> This verse says that Christ loved the church, and gave himself for it! Who is the church? The ecclesia---the called out ones! And Paul has made it clear in Ephesians 1 that they were chosen on the basis of God's will, and not on the basis of anything good in them, nor on the basis of their choice.

XIII THE SOVEREIGNTY OF GOD IN CALVINISM CHARTED IN COMPARISON TO OTHER VIEWS (Chapter 32)

See chapter 32, as it is difficult to summarize a chart.

XIV THE SOVEREIGNTY OF GOD IN SALVATION IN RELATION TO MAN'S WILL (Chapter 34)

A. **There is no doubt about it that the Bible teaches salvation is by the grace of God alone, and all true Bible believers will agree with that statement, though they may disagree in their definition of what it means!**

See Ephesians 2:8-9, Titus 3:5

B. The question then becomes, is man saved by grace, if he has the ability to exercise faith in Christ for salvation in his own strength and power, or would that be salvation by works?

C. The question then becomes, what effect did the fall leave on man regarding any spiritual ability to cooperate with God in the work of salvation?

See Ephesians 3:1, Romans 3:7-8, Jeremiah 17:9

D. Man is unworthy and God owes him nothing!

F. But what if God to glorify and display His grace determines to rescue some men from the power and penalty of sin?

XV THE SOVEREIGNTY OF GOD AND THE BAPTIST CONFESSIONS OF FAITH (Chapters 36-37)

The Second London Confession of Faith of 1689 and the Philadelphia Confession of Faith 1742 were both Baptist confessions of faith, which were very strongly Calvinistic and were influential on early Baptists in America.

The Second London Confession was a copy for the most part of the Westminster Confession of Faith and the Philadelphia Confession was a copy of the Second London Confession.

Therefore, it is beyond dispute that early Baptists in America were strongly Calvinistic in their doctrine.

As we went through this material, at least a condensed version of it, I took the first seven divisions and Dink took the last eight. They gave us three hours (surprise), and we each took all of that time, with a break in the middle. It was not our intention to convince them of our doctrine, but to at least show them two things:

1.   Our position was strongly based upon Scripture.
2.   Our position was firmly grounded in Baptist history.

As the presentation unfolded, I sensed we were making some gains among our listeners. First, our attitude was gracious and objective and academic. Second, our basis of information was Scripture and history. Third, Dink blew them away with his knowledge of the material---something they had never expected of him. Though they may have been surprised at my knowledge of theology, they at least expected me, as a teacher of theology, to know his stuff to some degree. But here was Dink, an old saved gang member from a mafia type background, and now a teacher of evangelism, who knew his theology as well as I did.

There was one sour grape in the bunch, however, and one could almost have guessed who it would be. But I think his attitude and reaction may have helped us, rather than hindering us. It was Larry Hollister. He insisted on a question at the end of my presentation, and I allowed him that. When I had answered his question with Scripture, he began to harangue me with silly emotional questions and arguments. I told him that what he said sounded good, but

I wanted him to show me some Scripture, which he couldn't or which he refused to do, whatever the case.

Then when Dink had finished, he did the same thing. But Dink tied him up in knots by giving him Scripture also, which he didn't seem to hear! And when Dink challenged him for Scripture, again, he could not give any. We were gracious and kind and patient, and he was edgy and harsh and more like an attack dog against us. And this point was very clear to the rest of the board.

Finally, Dr. Sisk thanked all the men for coming, and asked them to pray about the matter, and it was no secret what he was talking about. They all knew there would come a vote on us at the next scheduled meeting. Many of them thanked us for the informative presentation, but not Larry Hollister. Johnny Rafferty was especially friendly, and he even apologized for his friend, Larry Hollister. He said he heard of my difficult time with him, and asked me not to think he had sent him. He did realize a conversation, they had about the matter may have been the springboard which sent him after me, and for that he was very apologetic. He didn't realize that Larry might react in that manner.

When the room was cleared, Dr. Sisk was very grateful also. He just went on and on about how much theology Dink knew. He was even more amazed how Dink had spoken the most beautiful English he had ever heard in all his life, and for the whole of his presentation. This was something I had seen Dink do before! His vocabulary was beyond belief, as he had used many words that Dr. Sisk didn't even know and had never even heard!

By the time I got home, I was drained! It was in the Lord's hands now! Just as it always had been! But would you believe it, the phone rang! It was Larry Hollister!

Chapter 42

The very first thing that came out of Larry Hollister's mouth was, "I've got to see you!" He stated no reason, nor did he say when he wanted to see me. I tried to put him off till the next week, but he insisted that it had to be now! At this demand I could have come unglued.

"Pastor Hollister, I have tried to be patient with you, but you are making it very difficult! First, you come to my office and verbally assault me. Then you act like something less than a gentleman by going to Dr. Sisk about the meeting in my office, that you forced. Then you try to take over the meeting of the board this afternoon, or at least try to argue me down, instead of listening to an objective presentation of my beliefs with an open mind. Then you try to do the same with Dink. Do you realize what a fool you made of yourself in the meeting today? And now after such a tiring and wearying day, you have the nerve to call me at 7:00 in the evening, and insist on seeing me for who knows what purpose---is it only to assault me again? Can't whatever you have to say wait until next week?"

There was silence on the other end of the phone line, and I wondered if he had hung up on me.

"Pastor Hollister? Are you still there?" I asked, not knowing if I was talking to a dead line or a living person.

"Yes, I am still here!" he said, but then there was silence again.

"Well, what do you have to say for yourself!" I chided him. "Come on! Spit it out! I have better things to do than hang on the line with a man who doesn't know what he wants to say to me---only that he has to see me tonight!"

Finally he got it out, as he said sheepishly, "I want to apologize!" But it was almost so soft I couldn't hear it.

"You what?" I asked, wanting to force him to say it with volume and conviction.

"I said, I want to apologize!" he said the second time with a voice which I certainly heard. Somehow, I still didn't trust him, as it had been so difficult to say those simple words, "I want to apologize!"

"Well, can't it wait till next week?" I asked.

"I guess so, if that's the way you feel about it!" he said sharply, and then he hung up on me.

One has to wonder about the sincerity of an apology, which is made in such a rude manner. I raised the question as to whether his so-called apology was for his own sake, more than for the sake of the person he had offended. But then that raised the question, if he was apologizing for his own sake, what motivation was behind the actions of his supposed apology? To save his own face before the seminary board? To set me up, so he could say he had apologized, and I had not accepted it?

I remembered back to the days of the inerrancy battle, which our denomination faced, early in my ministry. The liberals were in control of the denomination, and they were so sweet and kind, promoting tolerance and graciousness for others, who might differ with them on their view of Scripture. We were supposed to rollover and play dead for them, as they controlled the denomination. But, then when the conservatives regained control of the convention, there was no tolerance call from them. They acted like their divine right to be in control had been taken away from them, and we were labeled as the intolerant ones.

The denomination had been in their control for a generation, and they acted like those who believed in verbal inspiration were interlopers, while their view had been the conviction of Evangelistic Baptists (our denomination) for the ages past, according to them. I concluded that must be the same way some men, even good conservative men, were now feeling about a return to the historic Baptist doctrinal roots of Calvinism. They had become so used to their Arminian doctrines of the present, and their Arminian methods of ministry, that they were convinced that this is what Baptists had always believed and practiced, when it was not, as a simple search of history would show!

Plus, when the revival of these doctrines began to take place, back in the mid-sixties, maybe they didn't think these truths would ever create much of a stir in our denomination. But when the number of those embracing these doctrines of grace increased in the 70's and 80's, some reacted, perhaps, knowing this was a revival of past Baptist doctrine, which they didn't want! Others were so shallow in their knowledge of history and doctrine, that they thought this was all something brand new for Baptists.

Many lay people were in that last category, because of their ignorance of Baptist doctrine and history. And that was what brought the idea that you are not "one of us." And they may be right, as one understands that such people are not in line with their own Baptist doctrinal heritage, while those of us who hold the doctrines of grace are!

Reformation (the return to the truth once delivered to the saints) is never an easy process. People are always very comfortable with their false ideas and doctrines. So it was during the Reformation in Europe, and so it will be for us!

May God help us to be faithful!

About this time, the phone rang again, and I thought, not again! Would Larry Hollister disturb me once more, or was it someone else?

At first I ignored it, but then I answered it, reluctantly!

Chapter 43

When I finally answered the phone, it wasn't Hollister, but it was Dink. Hollister had just called him with the story that he had tried to apologize to me, but I wouldn't accept his apology. According to his version of the story, I had been very rude to him, and that settled the issue in his mind. He would do his best to make sure that we would not be back next year, and we could go to the bank on it, because he had the backing of Dr. Sisk and the rest of the board. I told Dink that it sounded to me like a man out of control, who was blustering with exaggerated statements of threats, concerning matters over which he had no control. He surely did not control Dr. Sisk nor the whole of the board, especially after the show he had put on today in the board meeting.

"You's probly right, Preacha! I guess we jus' better leave it all in da Lord's hands, 'cause ole Hollister may very well self destruct on his own in da whole process!" Dink observed.

"Yes, if he hasn't already!" I added.

In the passing of the days prior to the crucial board meeting, we didn't meet with Dr. Sisk, so we couldn't get any read on his thoughts or position on the whole issue. Neither were we able to ask him or talk to him about Larry Hollister and what to expect at the board meeting. We were only informed that it would take place on the next Friday at 10:00 in the morning. We did get some feedback before then that Hollister had been busy politicking and even telling his story of my refusal to accept his apology.

Therefore, as Dink and I went to this meeting, we had no idea as to the format or what to expect. We sat down in the back of the conference room. I expected to be invited to leave at a certain point, so that they could discuss the matter in privacy before they voted. The meeting began with a devotional and prayer, and then Dink and I were asked if we had anything further to say. I replied in our behalf that we were willing to abide by the vote of the board, trusting God's providence and sovereignty in the board's final action.

Then, when the chairman rose and asked if there was anyone else who wished to speak prior to the vote concerning the motion before the board (the motion concerning our future there at the school), Dr. Sisk asked if he could be permitted to speak. Obviously there were no objections. He read from a prepared statement.

"Members of the Board of Trustees of Evangelistic Baptist Theological Seminary! I come before you today to try to put to an end something I myself started at the beginning of this school year! When I came to EBT I had many ideas concerning the needs and future of our school. I had some preconceived thoughts about two faculty members, one, who I had known twenty plus years ago as a student, and another I had only known from afar. I must say, I was not in agreement with the theology I heard that they held! This deeply concerned me!

"I came to this school, therefore, with the conviction that they and any others like them, because of their theological stance, needed to be removed as faculty members as soon as possible, especially since they had built such a strong following among the students. I was convinced that we could not go any further in allowing them and their doctrine to become entrenched in our school. So, I told the one professor, the one I knew the best, and who I had tutored on the various theological systems of theology earlier, while he was a student at

Baptist College, that he and the other man could begin making preparations to find other places of employment. I almost guaranteed him that this would be their last year on this campus.

"But I knew that in order to present the matter to the board, that I would need to build a case for their dismissal. This I did by instructing Dr. Welsh, the Dean of Faculty, to begin visiting their classes to see if we could build a case against them for dismissal on the grounds of their weakness in the area of their teaching and communicative skills. For various and obvious reasons, we came to a conclusion, that this approach would not work, because they are two of the best communicators on campus---just ask the students!

"I then asked Dr. Pointer to write a paper for me, and I intended to use that paper to build a case against them for dismissal on the grounds of their doctrine. Dr. Pointer suggested that we (including the second man also) meet one day a week for several weeks to discuss their doctrine, and this I agreed to do. But that is where I made my mistake!" he said with a smile. "It was in these weekly meetings that I began to see their hearts and also to understand their doctrine. But that was not the end of it.

"Somehow, I know not how and I will not ask even now, the plight and whereabouts of my wayward son came to their knowledge, and they by the help and grace of God were able to lead him to the Lord and bring him home to us! My wife and I now have a solid relationship with our long lost boy, and they even went further! They helped him, along with the aid of another friend of theirs, to make straight several things that were a total mess in his life.

"I trust you will understand what I am going to say now about the matter which brings us together today, that is, this vote for their dismissal from their teaching positions at this school. I know if I am not careful in my wording, that you could misinterpret this whole situation. Through this entire ordeal these two men have conducted themselves as Christian gentlemen. They have not engaged in politics over their situation. They have kept the student body calm, as somehow the students too came to know of this matter, not through them, but because of someone else on this campus, who was trying to play politics with their situation, and we will deal with that later, if that is God's will.

"But even further, I came to understand their doctrine and their hearts, as they acted and reacted throughout my whole relationship with them, and I am sure it was a great ordeal for them. I found out that they are in line with past Baptist history in what they are teaching, and that they were teaching their thoughts objectively, displaying a gracious and kind spirit towards those who disagree with them. They only desired an opportunity for these convictions to be presented in a fair and honest and objective manner. And isn't that true education?

"As you can see, I have changed completely in my stance towards them. I was wrong in my convictions concerning them. I was wrong in my desire to work to get them removed from the faculty of this seminary. And as I have wrestled with this issue, I have come to the conclusion that I must make this right with the Lord and with them.

"In order for me to make this right with them and God, I have come to the conclusion that I must do the following. I request that you put my name with theirs on your ballot of dismissal, as you take this vote in light of my sin in this whole situation. If you will not do that, then I will turn in my resignation now, for that is the only other thing I can do. I can leave with them or stay with them. We all three are now in this together."

Dr. Sisk then turned to us and said, "I do ask your forgiveness for my sin against you, and for the gloom of uncertainty that I placed upon your lives and the lives of your family members for these months. Thank you, for being Christian gentlemen, when I was not!"

Understandably, there was a deathlike calm, when he had finished and sat down, and as Dr. Sisk even broke into tears! I thought, not even Larry Hollister would dare say anything now---it was such a special and honest moment before God. God's presence flooded the place, as we should have expected, when sin is confessed, and when things are made right with God and others. Surely others of the board, maybe not all, had the same spirit of repentance concerning their previous attitudes towards us.

I noticed that even Dink had tears in his eyes, as did I! Then the chairman took the floor asked if there were any objections to adding Dr. Sisk's name to the list of dismissal, along with ours, and there were none. Then he asked if anyone else wished to say anything before the vote was taken. With that a voice rang out from the back of the room.

"I suppose its okay for me, the newest member of this board to say somethin'. I feel like the old boy who said some years ago that he'd been through three hangin's, a number of hog killins' and a lot of county fairs, but he ain't never seen nothin' like this fiasco of the last few weeks, since I became a member of this board of trustees!"

There was something strangely familiar about that voice and those figures of speech. It had to be our old friend, Jasper Showers, I thought, as I turned around and stretched to see who it was, remembering that he was the newest member of the board! (see *A Journey in Salvation*, Richbarry Press, 2001)

"I don't know who all you boys are!" he said addressing the board members. "But I'll guarantee you that Ma Bell never had as many phone calls as I have had these past few weeks with as much politickin' goin' on just tryin' to get me to vote these two men out of their positions here at this school. And most of you didn't know what you was talkin' about! Well, I hate to tell you men, but you're like a one-eyed dog in a chicken coop, and you need to get out of the coop and get back up on the porch where you belong, until you can see how wrong you were in this matter!"

You can understand the shock his words brought to the board. Jasper then told of how he was a pure Arminian in his doctrine, and how he thought he had lost his salvation, and how he was about to lose everything, including his family and ministry. Then he met "these two guys," who spent hours and hours working with him, helping him to understand the truth! He told them if it hadn't been for us, he would have lost everything, and that he was in the ministry today, because of the truth that we taught him.

Then he added, "And I think you have heard today that I ain't the only one who has been blessed by the lives and ministries of these two men of God!" referring to our ministry to Daryl Sisk. "If any of you vote against them today, after what you've heard about their lives and ministry, you're about as crazy as an old run-over dog. Just go and talk to your own student body!"

Following those blunt words, Jasper sat down, and the Chairman of the Board called for a vote by ballot. But one man rose, and I am not sure that what followed was in accordance with the proper parliamentary procedures according to Roberts rules of order, but no one seemed to object. The brother made a suggestion that the board remove the previous motion of dismissal from the floor of their meeting and that it be done by a standing vote of acclamation with apologies from the board to the two men who had suffered so much from the previous accusations.

Again, to my surprise, when the chairman asked if there was any objection to the suggestion of taking a visible standing vote on the matter instead of by a written ballot, there was none---not even Larry Hollister, who was seated a few rows ahead of us. Again, to my joy and surprise, when the chairman asked for all who favored the removal of the previous motion from the floor to show it by standing, everyone in the meeting stood, including Larry Hollister!

I guess we will never know what would have happened, if Dr. Sisk had not added his name to ours on the list, nor the impact of Jasper's blunt but direct words to the board. But it certainly was a variety of defenses for us---one gracious and kind and the other bold and blunt, along side of our defense the previous day! All seem to have been used of the Lord for the accomplishment of His purpose and will. I was positive, also, that the entire board of trustees had gained a new appreciation for the kind of man that they had leading their school in Dr. Sisk---a real man of God and a Christian gentleman! And also a respect for their newest board member in Jasper Showers---one able to summarize a situation in a nutshell by blunt and honest language! And, hopefully, there was also a better appreciation and understanding of two of their faculty members!

Postscript

**(A note by the author, Dr. Belcher, about himself and
the writing of this series of theological novels,
with special reference to this one!)**

I am often asked how much of the content and how
many of the events of these "journey" books really
happened to me in my experience in the ministry. I answer
that an author usually has three sources for his material. He
writes, out of his own experience; or, from what he has
seen taking place in the lives of others; or, even from the
wealth of possibility to be found in his own imagination.
So the answer to the above question is that some of these
events of the journey books did happen to me. Others I
have taken from the lives of those I have known in
ministry, perhaps with some embellishment, at times.
Many more are the product of my imagination, hopefully,
within the realm of possibility in the real life setting of a
pastor, a church, a family, or even a school.

I note the above to add that I did teach at a Christian
University for twenty-nine years. It was not a denominational school, but one with a pluralistic setting, which is to
say, we had students and faculty members there all the way
from five point Arminians to five point Calvinists! It was
quite a unique experience! All the time I was there, I
sought to be objective in my teaching (though I do think all
knew where I stood), and fair to the other viewpoints, and
loyal to the school itself in its pluralistic setting. I was not
there to argue or to convince people of my system of
theology, but to set forth, even as I taught theology, the
various views to be found within the evangelical setting of
the day and of the past. It was up to the Lord to do with my

teaching and His truth what He wished to do, and I remain satisfied that He did!

I say this so that no one will ever think that any of the plot of this book came from my experiences at the school where I taught. Absolutely not! I never felt any pressure while I was there concerning what I taught or how I taught! I never sensed any theological friction between the other faculty members and myself, or between myself and the administration. I look upon this school, as a sterling example of how God's people can come together from divergent theological backgrounds and work together in the training of young people for the service of the Lord, while possessing different theological beliefs within the setting of the major doctrines of evangelical theology.

On the other hand, it must be noted that teaching at a denominational school would be different, for usually such schools do have a well-defined doctrinal statement of a more narrow nature, which reflects the denomination's doctrine, not only in the major areas, but also in other areas. In simple words most denominations do not have a pluralistic doctrinal setting, but a denominational confession or statement of faith. And a teacher is committed to be faithful to the doctrines set forth in that document. But this is where the rub comes in, as schools begin to drift from their clearly stated historical doctrinal moorings, to the place where their theology becomes fuzzy and even altered from that which their statement of faith sets forth.

Such is the setting of this journey book, and such has been the history of some Baptist groups and their schools, as they drifted in the past from their original standards. And such is the struggle many have gone through to try to bring a denomination back to its doctrinal beliefs. Some

Baptist groups have seen victory over glaring liberalism within their ranks, a liberalism that had even denied the authority and inerrancy of the Bible. But with this victory settled, they turned to deny other Baptist brothers, who helped them in the inerrancy battle, the right to pursue the heritage of the denomination in its Calvinistic roots and confessional standards, as if Baptists never were Calvinists!

There has come and there does continue to be a revival of the Calvinistic heritage among Baptists. Fifty years ago there were very few Calvinists, but now they are everywhere! I suppose this is what frightens some people. Perhaps it is time for a warning to go out to both groups--- both the Calvinistic Baptists and the non-calvinistic Baptists. To the latter group I would warn, that if this revival of Calvinism among Baptists is of God, no one can stop it! Men may fight against us, even other sincere Baptists, whether it be out of ignorance of the past history of Baptists or out of their blind prejudice or misunderstanding of these doctrines, but God's truth will prevail. To the former group, the Calvinistic Baptists, I would say that we need to be gracious and loving and kind with a Christ-like spirit, being at the same time wise as serpents and harmless as doves, and yet strong in our convictions.

May we never lose sight of the ultimate goal of the Christian life, and that is to be like Christ, not only in the truth of our doctrines, but also in the tone and demeanor of our lives. How easy it is to overbalance to either side of that tension---sound doctrine with an ungracious spirit or a gracious spirit without a concern for the soundness of doctrine. May we be reminded that both of these extremes fall short of our Lord's desire for us, and can reek havoc upon His church as we seek to labor together.